About the Author

Born a pessimist in Edinburgh, Frank Valentine was orphaned as a baby, adopted and taken from the comparative safety of Scotland to some prime German targets in England, just in time for him to learn how to run before the bombs began raining down. Six terrifying years later the war ended, the nightmares took a little longer.

As a lad he learned the trumpet with the idea of picking up some extra money playing in one of the local palais, just in time for the dance orchestras to disband, all the dance halls to close down and guitar players to take over the planet.

He joined the Merchant Navy and was still sailing the seas and oceans of the world missing almost the entire groovy, swinging, free loving, permissive 1960s, invariably being stuck in the middle of nowhere on board ship, when, at the age of thirty-two, he met and married his wife in five weeks. Moving to rural Norfolk for peace and tranquillity, he discovered he'd married a woman who never stops talking.

THE FINAL YARN

Frank Valentine

THE FINAL YARN

AUSTIN MACAULEY
PUBLISHERS LTD.

A CIP catalogue record for this title is available from the British Library.

Although the characters in this publication are drawn from the author's wide experience, any precise resemblance to any real person, living or dead, is purely coincidental.

ISBN 978 1 78455 129 2

www.austinmacauley.com

Published (2014)
Austin Macauley Publishers Ltd.
25 Canada Square
Canary Wharf
London
E14 5LB

Printed and bound in Great Britain

Dedication

To my wife and family, the second for expanding.

To my G.P., Dr Jim Powell for keeping me alive.

And to the memory of Ernie Abbey, friend, shipmate, gentleman and incorrigible drunk, for being the most delightful of piss hounds.

Hear the yarn of a sailor
An old yarn learned at sea

John Masefield

Stand-By

The Old Man had recently started shaving; no one suspected why, only Tedward knew. Few, however, bothered commenting on the noteworthy improvement. His had been no run-of-the-mill beard but a shapeless, unkempt, prematurely grey mass covering his face in coarse abundance and partially obscuring his gnarled, scarlet nose and matching eyes which could burn into one like a blow-torch.

'Like a fuckin' ferret squintin' from a grizzly's arse'ole,' Drunken Duncan gleefully recalled.

Nor was he even old, but tradition being what it traditionally is, the Old Man he had become. Anyway, his menacing appearance had been decreased to a more acceptable level. The bloodshot eyes, however, having been cultivated by years of dedicated imbibition, had found permanent refuge.

His grammar school education in the Midlands had ended in sudden ignominy at the sensitive experimental age of fifteen, for reasons known only to himself, another strangely emotional boy from a lower form, his bewildered parents and a headmaster rendered speechless with horror. (This was, after all, the unenlightened thirties.) The hapless head had reluctantly composed an acceptable testimonial, only after being assured it would be used to send him away to sea, from which, God willing, he would never return.

Enrolment into a training establishment for merchant navy officer cadets was hurriedly arranged and time hung heavy with embarrassment as prayers were sent up for his speedy departure. They both dutifully accompanied him to the station, more as a military escort than a farewell duo. As the lad stood ignored, by his suitcase, they paced in agitated anticipation of those awaiting the results of the last two lottery numbers with either the possibility of a substantial or gigantic win on the cards. At last the train arrived. Mother mewed and heaved, dabbing dry eyes as father blinked rapidly, solemnly shaking his head before turning dramatically away to blow his nose.

The whistle sounded and the train moved slowly off bearing the disconsolately waving youngster into the smoky distance, towards a new life for which he had no particular desire.

In contrast, his relieved parents *did* have a particular desire and were looking forward to new beginnings as far removed from their present location as possible. Understandably apprehensive that full knowledge of their begotten boy's incomprehensible behaviour would soon spread furtively throughout the neighbourhood, not a moment had been wasted and a buyer was found for their home of many a contented year.

An astute gambler in the stock markets, his father had acquired a substantial stake in a company of condom manufacturers which looked like affording the bemused couple genteel respectability throughout the years to come. Understandably elated with the financial wisdom exercised in birth control he, nevertheless, was filled with deep sorrow that he had lacked the foresight to practise it to the letter.

Initially they assured each other that it was only a question of time before they wrote to the boy informing of their whereabouts, but neither had the slightest intention of so doing, and never did.

En route to the metropolis and his future, the luckless lad, Tedward on his knee, gazed with damp, sightless eyes at junctions, signal boxes, grimy sheds and stationary rolling stock passing ever faster beyond the window, blessedly unaware of developments at home. Which was just as well for the Pickford van was at the door loading furniture and effects for a journey even more distant than his own, only in the opposite direction.

Pre-sea training satisfactorily completed, he joined a company of general cargo vessels, the Whippit-Snide Line.

During only his second day of service tragedy struck when his ship, the *Rose Snide*, vanished forever into the murky English Channel after colliding with an oil tanker, and he became officially listed as missing.

In the company's Leadenhall Street head office, Sir Reginald Whippit-Snide, Bart., had hastily convened an urgent board meeting. His opening lamentations of grief and sorrow at having summoned members so hastily from home, club and mistresses' arms, gave way to an air of muted enthusiasm, which caught their full attention.

'Gentlemen,' he began, 'I have received a call from Athens. There is a replacement vessel laid up, ready and waiting.' He paused thoughtfully before continuing in a paternal manner. 'I believe, however, that an appropriate period should elapse... y'know... mark of respect... that sort of thing...'

'Hear, hear!'

'Until Lloyd's acknowledges our claim, which ... incidentally was lodged immediately on learning of this... er... tragic affair.'

Heads nodded in solemnity and he squared his jaw. 'I am, of course, confident that the inquiry's findings into the cause of this... er... calamity will attach no blame whatever to the good name of Captain... er... whatever his good name was, and that the Line's reputation will remain untarnished.'

He smiled benevolently during the ripple of appreciation and pressed on.

'After all, gentlemen, the other ship wasn't British y'know. Good Lord no! She was a foreign tub... one of those notoriously unseaworthy Greek outfits... probably straight from a damned lay-up yard. Her owners won't have a leg to stand on.'

(More applause.) Sir Reg was grinning now.

'I must inform you, gentlemen,' he continued, suppressing a chuckle, 'that there is one very acceptable facet to this... er... distressing situation... out of adversity and all that... yes indeed. There is little logic or business sense in our acquiring a newer ship or even one on a par with the poor old Rose, when it looks as though the Germans... naughty devils...' (laughter) 'will be sending her to the bottom before much longer.' He was warming to the subject nicely, ably assisted by appropriate atmosphere.

'Such being the case, gentlemen,' he went on, happily, 'a substantial sum from the settlement will be retained by us after the purchase.'

This was indeed music to the ears of the privileged gathering, many of whom could trace their ancestry back to privileged apes. Their vigorous appreciation filled the room. The revered chairman and managing director held a manicured hand aloft.

'As you are aware, gentlemen, should war ensue, merchant shipping may well be placed under Admiralty control. As proud and loyal subjects we shall willingly make the sacrifice in order to beat the Hun, for victory will ensure compensation of a scale enabling us to enlarge the fleet, with which to help in the re-building of Europe...'

An unprecedented roar engulfed him and he arose to savour it the better.

...'*maybe even half the world*!' he cried, '*if we're lucky*!'

They cheered, slapped the table, stamped and whooped ecstatically. Not until he thought he'd heard the last '*Bravo*' did he bring the meeting to a close.

While such matters of significance took place, bodies were being washed ashore in grim delivery by the incoming tide. On the day following, with the lifting fog, a fishing vessel nosed into Brixham harbour with her catch, which included an officer cadet who had stubbornly clung to the nets and also to a hairy, ginger object not easily recognizable as a teddy bear. As funeral arrangements for shipmates he had barely known were being initiated, he was borne ashore for weeks of recuperation and weeks of wondering why letters sent home remained unanswered.

There were then five ships in the Whippit-Snide Line – the *Mary Snide*, being the first acquired after the death of Sir

Reg's favourite aunt, followed by receipt of her astronomical legacy. Then came the *Anne Snide*, named after his first wife, and the *Daisy Snide* after his second. The *Jane Snide*, named after his third wife was hastily re-named *Lady Snide* following a baronetcy gained through the good offices of his father-in-law. The *Vyvyn K Snide* was named after his son. The ill-fated *Rose Snide* had been a tribute to his mother.

War came as prophesied and wily German U-boats sent British merchant shipping to the seabed with alarming regularity. This systematic destruction of Britain's lifeline to the world beyond soon displayed a curious fact. Although old, slow and vulnerable, the Whippit-Snide fleet was enjoying remarkable good fortune. It was soon assumed in high and mighty places that the enemy deemed them unworthy of expending ammunition on. In consequence they were snapped up for assignments vital to the nation, like transporting whisky to the United States and film stars for Hollywood.

There was always a berth for Sir Reg's friends in the aristocracy. His elevation to their ranks had reached only the bottom rung.

The Old Man, of solitary disposition since school days, did not change noticeably. He rarely spoke unless addressed, which was rare because he rarely spoke to anyone. Broodingly he'd sit drinking alone in dockland bars. On board he dined in the saloon with the other officers, where his presence was resented. The engineers loathed him simply because he was a cadet deck officer and the deck officers despised him, mistaking his moody silence for a driving, single-minded ambition which they found intolerable for they all craved eventual command in the diminishing merchant fleets. Not surprisingly, when he became third mate at the age of twenty-one, he was viewed with suspicious contempt.

At the end of the war his drinking had worsened, which did not arouse undue concern for his duties were performed meticulously. His judgement on every aspect of his job was beyond reproach; he studied his appointed tasks with grim determination and his sea watch was diligence itself as he shouldered his growing responsibilities. Rest periods were spent poring over textbooks while pouring out drinks. He was soon the proud owner of a first mate's certificate, followed by promotion to second mate of the *Anne Snide*. It was here that he acquired an unfortunate smear on his reputation.

Angus McKenzie, the *Anne Snide's* second engineer at that time, was an extremely bad loser, which was evident as he left the spark's cabin ungraciously slamming the door behind him. En-route to his quarters, a reflection caught his eye, stopping him abruptly beyond the reclusive second mate's door, which was open. Eagerly but cautiously he peered inside from around the bulkhead, his card game completely forgotten.

'Jesus Christ!' he whispered, jaw dropping in astonishment beneath gaping eyes. On his way again, a vicious grin divided a face glowing with malice. 'Well, ah'll go t'holy hell!'

To be in possession of such verbal weaponry was very gratifying and the thought that he might be its sole possessor was bordering on ecstasy. Oh what fucking joy! The chief must be informed without delay. This would greatly enhance the engineers' arsenal in the perpetual feud against deck officers, *of which he was the most fervent supporter*.

* * *

'Captain' announced Sir Reg, striding briskly through the door, having breezed up from London to meet the ship when docked in Hull, 'I have reason to believe your second officer is indulging in practices which, I have reason to believe, could jeopardize the reputation of the Line, making it even more difficult to recruit the type of officer of the calibre, I have reason to believe, we deserve.'

'But wha...?' managed the alarmed master, very startled indeed by the sight of the company 'god' on board his ship. He'd only ever set eyes on him once before and that from a distance. He was obviously not meant to speak because Sir Reg ignored him.

'If he does not pledge forthwith to discontinue this unmanly behaviour, I shall dispense with the services of this infernal fellow on the spot.' Sighing self-righteously he blusteringly added 'Dammit all…! We'll be the laughing stock of the high seas!' He then breezed away.

Unbeknown to the chairman, his son, Vyvyn K, who'd accompanied his father on the trip from head office, had become readily acquainted with the *Anne Snide's* second mate. From their first meeting they had chattered happily together and soon wild whores wouldn't have dragged them apart.

Before leaving for London, Sir Reg became aware of the enchantment 'twixt his boy and the second mate and made a mental note to assist the career of this sociable officer. He also derived particular relish in bawling-out the chief engineer from whom he had received the defamatory telegram, which he clearly now saw as a disgusting lie… Conversing with a teddy bear, indeed! None of *his* officers could do such a thing. He would have revelled in firing the malignant old meddler but the company had a difficult enough job already recruiting engineers of the calibre they had reason to believe they deserved.

The following years saw the Old Man serving competently on each of the 'Snide' vessels, except the *Mandy Snide*, a post war addition and named after Sir Reg's dog, on which his health deteriorated alarmingly. After prolonged and agonizing bouts of diarrhoea, resulting in dramatic weight loss, he had taken to his death bed where he was visited personally by the chief steward bearing bowls of what he called 'hot nourishing soup', which only made matters worse. Despite this, at twenty-nine, he gained his master mariner's certificate and promotion to first officer.

As second-in-command he was directly responsible for the day-to-day duties of the bosun and the deck hands, a job that he tackled zealously. He made his vessel the smartest in the fleet, with the utmost efficiency, and soon every 'Whippet Snide' master was glancing over his shoulder and anxiously contemplating his future, for none were ignorant of the rumour linking him with the influential son and heir. Whereas, in reality, Vyvyn K was far too artistic and intellectual, even snobbish, to want anything more than a passing acquaintance with the sea-going personnel. But rumours being what they are, they flourished in the fertile environment of anxiety.

Thus did he serve for another six years until Captain Arbuckle, respected master of the *Sarah Snide*, conveniently expired in Montevideo. *At last he had arrived, Captain Crawley Bix.* Being flown out from leave to assume his first command, still only in his mid-thirties and the youngest master in the fleet, did nothing to scotch the rumours. He hated flying but had been obliged to do so occasionally and accepted it with reluctance, having idly noticed that the happiest people in airports were those who had just disembarked.

At Montevideo harbour, he lovingly surveyed the lines of the *Sarah* of which he was the undisputed master – lord of his floating domain. Once in his quarters he bellowed for a drink. Stanley Stone, the chief steward, appeared, ill at ease, for he'd seen him come aboard. His resemblance to Stan Laurel was even more evident today because his face was as white as a sheet.

'Whisky, sir?' he stammered, bottle in hand.

'Tell me...' asked the Old Man, whose eyes had narrowed and were fixed on him.

'Have we sailed together before?'

'B... before... sir?' The bottle neck rattled on the rim of the glass as he poured nervously with long, slim hands. 'I... er... really don't er... know.'

'I believe we have.'

'I... er... cannot recall... sir,' he whispered, averting his eyes, as the Old Man's bored into his frightened skull. Knocking back two glasses and demanding instant replenishment, the Old Man grinned, humourlessly. 'I... er...', the steward stammered on, '...think I can... er... recall all the captains under whom I've served... sir.'

'I was not a captain then.'

'Oh.'

Draining his scotch, the Old Man toyed with the glass, asking matter-of-factly, 'Were you ever on the Mandy?' He sniggered maliciously as the steward almost dropped the bottle.

'No... I... er...'

Leering with loathing, the Old Man recalled the oily voice and the hot, far from nourishing soup, and the steward squirmed.

'Look... er... sir,' he bleated, anxious to remove himself from this fearful discomfort. 'I really can't stand... er ... here... all day... sir. I have much to... er do b...before we... er sail, sir.'

'Mmmmmm,' murmured the Old Man, with ill-concealed disappointment. He was beginning to enjoy inflicting this whisky-assisted torment. Still... he had plenty of time. 'Oh, very well,' he sighed, chuckling silently as Stanley Stone scuttled hurriedly away.

Next morning the officers assembled for breakfast, the Old Man arriving last, his face discoloured from his night of solitary intemperance and bags like scrotal sacks under his glowering red eyes. There were also the beginnings of the beard that would keep him hidden from the world for fourteen years. He had slept fitfully, dreaming of a visit to the crew's quarters in the stern where he'd logged all hands a week's pay to demonstrate his authority. They had reacted by lashing both him and Tedward to the drum of a winch, subjecting them to every known humiliation.

'Morning gentlemen,' he grunted, taking his seat at the head of the table. Stanley Stone timidly made introductions, although the Old Man was not unknown to some. They ate in silence, save for the clinking of cutlery, as furtive, uneasy glances periodically darted his way. Only the eyes of chief engineer, Angus McKenzie, remained defiant.

The Old Man retained command of the *Sarah* until she was resold to the Greeks for scrap, when he was transferred, along with Angus and Stanley, to the *Susan Snide*. This was the company's latest, most modern acquisition, the pride of the fleet – flagship of the Line.

Her present voyage was nearly over and only two ratings were re-signing. One was the cook, a small, rotund Cornishman, pillar of the 'Flat Earth Society' and a Field Marshal in the Cornish Liberation Army. He had a short left leg and a hump on his back in which he smuggled ship's stores ashore. The other was Drunken Duncan who, for the first time, was being allowed to make two consecutive trips on the same ship.

The only officers not re-signing were the fourth engineer and a deck cadet who was being dispensed with because he was an ex-grammar schoolboy who had not been expelled. The Old Man would not tolerate this and longed to rid himself of Hercules Duff, the first mate, a pious and noticeable Christian, who read the Bible daily and attended services all over the world. He was introverted, passive, gentle and unassuming, seeing goodness even in those completely lacking any. He could remain unruffled in the most stressful situations, radiating kindness, understanding and forbearance towards all and the Old Man hated his devout, imperturbable guts. He was not opposed to religious convictions providing people didn't take them seriously, believing man was made in God's image because man invented him.

An air of impending doom hung over Custom House E.16 as the *Susan Snide* headed for the Royal Docks to unload and sign on new crew. The signing-on seemed to be the root of the despondency and certain wily seamen, although desperate for work, deemed it wise to make themselves scarce by various ploys until she was underway again.

II

In the saloon on Saturday evening, the officers of the *Judith Snide* were being entertained by their counterparts on board the Susan at her berth in the Royal Albert Dock. The Old Man disliked the custom which took place whenever two 'Snide' vessels were in port together – that the first to arrive played host to the second.

He wandered, scowling behind his whiskers, as he liberally refilled various glasses. The sooner they had all consumed their rations, the sooner they would get to hell off his ship. But it was close to midnight and neither Captain Anderson nor his companions looked likely to depart.

The visiting chief engineer's wife was present and the Old Man, grasping every opportunity, endeavoured to accelerate her gin consumption so that her raucous spouse would have to end his partying to carry her off.

'Another drink? Another drink?' he hopefully enquired, approaching with the bottle.

'Well maybe just a little,' had been her standard reply all evening, smiling sweetly, invariably protesting but not vigorously, at his generosity.

'Nonsense, my dear, nonsense,' he would retort heartily. 'Drink up. Drink up.' He would then head for more empty glasses, leaving her to do so with increasing speed as the night wore on. Had he made a closer study of the only female present, he may have observed that her lustrous eyes reflected anticipation of more than gin.

The dutiful wife had journeyed from Barrow-in-Furness to be re-united with her husband after months apart, but her unflinching gaze of unbridled sensuality was being completely ignored by her revelling mate. So eventually her gin-motivated, deep, misty pools of longing altered course towards the Old Man who had spent much time hovering around her.

Initially, being totally inexperienced in such matters, comprehension was as far off as the dawn. Slowly and insidiously it arose from his subconscious, as from a bank of cloud, and he felt oddly uncomfortable. Awareness was clarifying midst the mist, however, then, with electrifying suddenness, broke through with a stupefying flash that sent him reeling and gasping. Unsteadily turning away from her pointed stare, he sought refuge out on deck, beneath the autumn moon.

The apprehension within kept the chill night air at bay. He

leaned heavily on a rail, his anguished mind wishing he were safely at sea but also contemplating (and being duly appalled at doing so) the lady's undoubted physical attributes. He gazed at the moon, unintentionally pondering the female mystery. The opposite sex was something he had spent his life avoiding. With his career, this had not been difficult so never before had he been subjected to such penetrating gaze and that oh-so-purposeful gleam under which he had shrivelled – suffused and benumbed – causing tremors deep within the solid old foundations of subconscious suppression.

Dabbing his furrowed brow, eyes closed in sad bewilderment, his head shook slowly and his cheeks despairingly inflated, forcing, in a sigh of resignation, a passage between closed lips. Oh, dammit all! Dammit all! They were just flesh and blood like everyone else, weren't they? Only with certain anatomical differences which had never before concerned him... Hey! Wait a minute! Never *before*...? Was he now...?

No... No... He gripped the rail with determination. No... indeed no, *definitely*. No sacrificial dupe, he, assuredly not. Why... they actually stank! Why else would they douche themselves in their blasted perfumery if not to hide something even more nauseating? Why else would Boots the chemist have a 'Female Hygiene' counter? Naturally, there was no call for a male one.

But why this sensation... the unfamiliar panic? Did she have designs on him? A word indecently exposed itself. Swallowing hard, his eyes shut even tighter as, by sheer willpower, he forced it away... but it forced its way back. Sex... Sex...

SEXUAL DESIGNS! He slumped over the rail, insides churning, shuddering at the thought when, eyes shooting open like greyhound traps, he became alert, suddenly aware of movement behind him. His heart lurched, his jaw sagged as he quickly straightened, spinning round, instantly rendering the lady in question unconscious as his flying elbow caught her squarely and resoundingly on the chin.

'Ohhhh NO... NO... CHRIST!' he wailed aloud, instinctively catching her before she hit the deck. 'What in the name...?'

Dazedly he held her evening-dressed slim form in his arms like twinkling sequinned drapes, dejectedly thinking how stupid he must look, like a second hauling the loser back to his stool. Suppose the inebriated husband appeared... Oh my God! Trembling, he bundled her over his shoulder and ascended discreetly, via the boat deck, to his personal quarters. Moving Tedward aside, he eased her onto his daybed, then dropped heavily into a chair, panting hoarsely, before snatching open a drawer to grab the medical book within.

He would normally, by now, have been feeling the effects of his own consumption of alcohol but shafts of enlightenment had smashed through the mist and now the terror of impending doom had usurped all.

'Loosen tight clothing,' he read, and accordingly removed her shoes and undid the top button of her gown. He waited expectantly as if having just performed some magical feat. She did not stir. Was she wearing anything tight underneath? What in blazes do they wear underneath, anyway? He had no idea.

'You'll have to find out, won't you,' prompted Tedward, propped up on his pillow. He had talked to Tedward at intervals throughout his years of excessive drinking and was not in the least surprised when he began to reply. Indeed, he seemed to have acquired independent mobility, as he did not seem always to stay where left.

'Er... wah... what d'ya mean?'

'It's obvious, man.'

'Er... obvious?'

'Look Crawley...,' the Old Man had graciously allowed Tedward to use his first name on occasions, but then, Tedward did what he liked anyway. 'You have no choice.'

'No choice... explain?'

'You'll have to find out by looking.'

With trembling fingers he touched her midriff and gently felt her abdomen and the relief was evident – he had found no foundation garment. Well, he thought, returning to his chair, passing a weary hand across his brow, I've done all I can do...

But suppose... just suppose, mark you... for argument's sake, she is wearing something tight. How will I know if I don't look properly?

'Precisely,' said Tedward, nodding understandingly.

'Oh hell!' the Old Man wailed, sweat beading his brow. He unzipped the gown and, lifting first one end of her and then the other, carefully slid it down over her long, shapely legs. This accomplished little for she wore a slip, which he almost ripped off in frustration. Ah! Now he was getting somewhere... those suspenders were far too tight. No sooner had he removed them, when Tedward cried excitedly...

'Look at her bra! See how tight it is!'

'Wha...? The Old Man, blinking through the sweat, threw off his jacket and loosened his tie. The heat was becoming unbearable. 'But my God!' he gasped, 'there must be a bloody limit to all this!' Shaking his head, he declared, 'this has gone far enough. I'm doing no more.' Turning on his heel, he made straight for the scotch.

'But you *must*!'

'Well I'm not.'

'Her bra is far too tight and...'

'*I don't damn-well care!*' he cried, flopping into the chair and draining a glass in one go.

'Listen...'

'*No! No! No!*' he exploded, 'there has to be a *limit*, do you HEAR?' Of this he was convinced. His jaw squared resolutely as he refilled the glass. He had done all he could... all he *would*. Absolutely nothing more would he contemplate. She could die for all he cared... What...? He sat bolt upright... Christ Almighty! NO!

'That *would* be the bloody limit,' smirked Tedward, reading his mind again, as the Old Man leapt up and fumbled with the fastenings. Grimly his damp, anguished face turned aside; he whipped the garment from her pale, peeping breasts, forcing himself not to peep back. They trembled like cherry-topped vanilla blancmanges, but he had returned to the whisky and his chair in which he swivelled around to stare disbelievingly at nothing in particular.

'Oh, what more can I *do*?' he wailed, wondering whether the other guests, her husband in particular, had missed them.

'You must think of something,' Tedward advised, 'and fast... she can't stay here all night.'

The Old Man, groaning in despair, struggled to his feet, where he wobbled, determinedly subduing his panic. Zombie-like, he lumbered towards the motionless body and, with a huge attempt at boldness, forced his half-open, bleary eyes to focus on her face. Oh, why did she not awaken? His troubled vision slid over her shapely breasts, coming to rest on where the elastic of her green, flimsy panties clung to her smooth abdomen. He quickly realized where his thoughts had wandered and dropped heavily to his knees, hirsute face in trembling hands, sobbing piteously.

'I won't do it... I... c...*can't*!'

'Of course you can,' Tedward retorted in phoney sympathetic encouragement. 'Just close your eyes and think of England.'

'Fuck bloody England!'

'Now, now, get a grip, Crawley, that kind of language is for ratings and engineers.' The Old Man knew he was right and momentarily, anyway, calmed somewhat.

'I'm sorry Tedward,' came the remorseful rejoinder, 'but put yourself in *my* position...'

'Like fuck, I will.'

'She must wake up! She MUST!' He looked up, suddenly, determined in fresh resolve. 'I'll bloody well MAKE her!' He made a sudden grab for her long, blonde hair and screamed in wide-eyed horror as it came off, revealing short, brunette curls. Flinging it angrily away as if fished from a contagiously contaminated bilge, he returned to his bottle, nostrils flaring, shaking his head in disbelief.

'Those panties look dangerously tight!' broke in Tedward, 'I said those...'

'I damned well hear you,' the Old Man snarled. He hated losing his cool with Tedward. He could not remember life without him. Then, as the thought struck him, he reached again for the medical book. No... he had not misread it. 'Loosen all tight fitting...' How in the world does one loosen panties? Oh Jesus!

'Precisely,' said Tedward helpfully, then his voice became shrill with urgency. 'Look man! Look! She's breathing with some difficulty!'

Agitated to every extremity, the Old Man shot to his feet and, shaking uncontrollably, slobbering in fear, he somehow managed to lift her legs high into the air and, shutting his eyes again, and thinking of England, yanked the tiny garment from her slender lower limbs. He staggered back to the whisky, drained like a kosher chicken.

'Ohhhhhhh! Christ have mercy!' he cried, slumping into his chair.

'You must do more,' urged Tedward mercilessly.

'I won't!' he snapped. 'I *won't*'. He would end this nightmare by biting the end of his tongue or pressing the tops of his eyeballs.

'But listen...'

The Old Man once more rested his weary head in his hands, too physically and emotionally fatigued to argue, as his whole body shook.

'Why,' he asked, brokenly, 'after years of stony, bloody silence, did you have to start *talking*?'

'But it's for her benefit that...'

'Oh... please... leave me alone...!'

'She is in need of...'

'AhhhhhEEEEEE!' the Old Man screamed, biting the end of his tongue and pressing the tops of his eyeballs.

'All right,' said Tedward, curtly, 'I'll rephrase that... It is not for her benefit, but yours.' He watched smugly as the Old Man's head rose, puzzled.

'Er... what...?' he began, blinking away the sweat. 'What in blazes do you mean? You're not making bloody sense.'

'Must I spell it *out*? Should misfortune befall the lady... here... on your daybed... naked? *The News of the World*?'

The Old Man was on his feet at once. Tedward *was* making bloody sense. 'What else can I do?' he wailed, and Tedward exclaimed in alarm.

'*Look*! I can no longer detect respiration. Her face is becoming pale...'

With a bound he was at her side, blind with fright. There was no way out. He could almost hear the metal doors clanging shut behind him. Surfing a wave of nausea and wringing his hot, sweaty hands, he bent over her glistening, unblemished nakedness, taking a deep breath as he did so. Then, in mid-bend he froze instantly. Had he detected slight movement of an eyelash? Had he read somewhere that women can use this unconscious trick as a ploy to get...?

On both counts he was dead right. Only fractionally before the scenario clarified, like a swift, coiling, deadly tentacle, her arm enwrapped his neck while the other had him expertly debagged in five seconds flat... a low throaty growl escaping her now panting lips. She had much more than mouth-to-mouth on her mind and had waited long enough already.

* * *

There were only about two guests left in the saloon when he returned at about two o'clock, looking much younger, minus his beard, and with a newly acquired step in his stride. Those of his officers who had not gone on leave had taken to their beds leaving only the visiting sparks and an engineer, neither of whom knew him well enough to notice any difference and saw nothing amiss at being greeted civilly. He strode around, a gleam in his eye and was genuinely disappointed when they too departed. The lady had long since left with her husband and his mind was now struggling betwixt unaccountable turmoil and likewise serenity.

Her frenzied attempts at sweaty coupling had failed – hardly surprising considering his state of mind – but in spite of this, certain unilateral action of a premature nature had culminated in amazing, shuddering cargo discharge, as he, like a member of Harry Houdini's audience, trembled and gaped in wide-eyed wonder.

Never in that old, be-whiskered million years would he have thought that a woman could so affect him. Deeply entrenched adolescent guilt and subsequent subconscious suppression had cruelly cocooned him from such kaleidoscopic delights. It was as if emotions had momentarily surfaced for a brief glimpse above the alcoholic lake. Tedward had revelled in his ringside seat and could find no fault with the Old Man's next idea.

* * *

Not long after the East End sparrows had begun croaking their madrigals into the industrial smog, Hercules Duff was bidding a moist farewell on a suburban platform.

'Oh dearest,' he whispered, 'I wish I could remain in your arms forever.'

'What? Here on the platform?' replied the vicar's wife in a soft West Country burr endeavouring to lighten the heavy atmosphere, for she too was very sad. 'Hold me ever closer, darling,' she urged, crestfallen at hearing the approaching train. She was not unpleasing to the average eye and wore a bejewelled cross around her neck, hanging outside her blouse in proud display. Their embrace had already caused consternation to other sleepy-eyed members of the travelling public and when pelvic regions began to bump and grind in abandoned unison, they had acquired a wide area all to themselves.

The two years seemed twice that in the suffering of his position as chief mate of the *Susan Snide*. On countless occasions he had almost applied for transfer, but fear of retribution from the Old Man, who apparently enjoyed close connections at head office, had prevented him from doing so. Not that he hated the Old Man. He was a Christian and, as such, merely harboured an intense dislike for the foul livered, degenerate, desolate, malevolent, cantankerous, naughty, naughty fellow. The comfort of his faith, to which he unashamedly clung, had been his mainstay throughout the ordeal. He worried constantly that the ratings found the spectacle of the Old Man reeling, stinking of booze, while he prayed, a source of unbridled amusement and had an indescribable dread that just mentioning this depraved addiction in the same breath as his private supplications would mysteriously undermine their potency.

* * *

In the *Kent*, the second cook and baker, quietly sipped brown ale as he watched the cook, with whom he'd not previously sailed, hopping about selling ladies underwear and toiletries to the exclusively male, yet colourful assembly.

'Do you have a light for me darling?'

Obligingly, he offered his Ronson as a cigarette, held between long, slim fingers, arced elegantly toward pouting red lips before sweeping to draw from the flame. With a barely audible 'thank you dear', the smoker eyed him expectantly through curling smoke before drifting away.

In Custom House, the Freemasons' jukebox strained to make an impact above the noisy gathering. Disconnected snatches of song had broken out and a party of Highland men patriotically bawled 'Lovely Stornaway' while another group rendered, to the tune of 'She'll be comin' round the mountain',

'Oh the chief he was a bugger in Mobile,

Oh the chief he was a bugger in Mobile,

Oh the chief he was a bugger

And the captain was another,

And they buggered one another in Mobile.'

The crew's mess was coming to life as they appeared on board in ones and twos, cold, hungry and clutching the inevitable carryouts of bottles and cans. There was no food in the hotpress which didn't work and sleep was not practicable as most would soon be required for duty. Drunken Duncan had been aboard since about nine, having been found asleep in the vandalised telephone box outside the 'Flying Angel' mission. He was now snoring in Suitcase Larson's bunk where Hard Nut Neilson and Oddball McCall had unwittingly dumped him. Shore leave expired at midnight and the vessel would sail for Hamburg at 0230 hrs.

On the fo'c'sle head, Hercules Duff pulled his hood more snugly around his ears and pocketed his hands, turning away from the icy wind that whipped across the deck and musing whether he would ever again set eyes on the vicar – his lover's husband. This he thought unlikely as his health was in rapid decline and some form of carcinoma was suspected. The devout clergyman had placed his well-being in the hands of God instead of doctors and had refused to be x-rayed. Hercules was experiencing moments of guilt for not being too displeased with the situation but then forced his thoughts to the matter in hand. Glancing impatiently as his watch, he wondered if the second mate was suffering similar delays at the stern. Two tugs stood by, one fore and one aft, their skippers swinging their arms and cursing the cold.

'They're all 'ere, chief,' the bosun announced, materialising like Merlin and followed by an unsteady bunch of stragglers, hidden from view beneath layers of clothing. The mate was extremely angry.

'All of you listen to me,' he ordered when they'd assembled. 'If you think that I'm going to tolerate this laxity you can jolly-well think again!' He stamped his foot for emphasis. 'So *there*!' he added, but continued stamping his foot because it was numb with cold.

The petty officers, bosun, carpenter and engine-room storekeeper were lucky to be aboard at all. After leaving the 'Stepps' in alcoholic effervescence, they had been imitating a chorus line, arms securely linked together, tunefully recalling a number from their long lost youth. During an unnecessarily extravagant display of choreography, they had misjudged the width of the quay and danced themselves into the dirty, stagnant dock.

Below, all preliminaries were complete. A full head of steam on both boilers impatiently awaited escape while, in the stern, the steering motor chugged healthily in readiness for its task of turning the rudder. All below gave a start as the shrill bell signalled the first manoeuvre of the voyage. As the inner dial spun to 'Slow Astern', the outer was manually positioned according to orders from the bridge. The fourth engineer spun the reversing gear into place and opened the steam control valve. The crank and shaft of the triple expansion engine began to turn.

Up on deck, fore and aft, steam winches rattled amidst clouds of vapour from glands and joints as they hauled aboard boxing-glove thick mooring ropes. With a thankful shudder, the *Susan Snide* carefully slid, stern first, the length of Albert Dock. Toiling tugs hustled her through the first swing bridge into the King George V Dock.

There she was brought about to face another, beyond which lay the lock, and then the Thames.

Dead Slow Ahead

The Old Man was performing a task he found not displeasing. He sat at his desk in Hamburg, the logbook threateningly open before him. The bosun and engine-room storekeeper, neither of whom looked very healthy after their impromptu ducking in the freezing Albert Dock, stood dutifully but unsteadily beyond the office door.

'Alright,' called the Old Man, 'bring 'em in one at a time.'

The bosun entered with a deckhand. 'McNiel, sir,' he croaked, with difficulty.

'Ah!' the Old Man exclaimed, 'I have here, McNiel,' he tapped the page with a forefinger, 'that you were adrift all yesterday. Is that correct?'

Big Deal McNiel shrugged indifferently.

'Suppose so, sir.'

'No suppose about it. Either you were adrift or you weren't.'

'I was.'

'Oh, thank you,' said the Old Man sarcastically. 'Would it be indiscreet to tell me where you went?'

'Just around.'

'Just around?'

'Yeah.'

'Is that all you've got to say?' The Old Man's disappointment showed. He'd expected to be inwardly amused by some wildly implausible excuse. Disappointment became anger. 'Just *around*?' he snapped. 'Suppose the cook went adrift and there was no food. You'd soon start complaining then.'

'Not judgin' by the grub so far, Cap'n.'

'Bah!' he growled, with an impatient gesture. 'You lot are

34

never bloody satisfied. No one will ever hear *me* complain about the fare aboard.'

McNiel could not dispute this, having heard that the Old Man existed almost entirely on alcohol, but wisely decided just to mutter, 'No sir.'

The Old Man sank back with a thankful sigh. For a moment there he feared being told that the reason he would never complain about the food was because he existed almost entirely on alcohol.

'Where were you anyway?' he snarled, then answered himself. 'On the damned piss I imagine, or with some filthy Jerry bitch.'

The Old Man had a lot to thank the Germans for, especially their U-boat commanders, but he was not the grateful sort and felt that after having in excess of twenty five million of their comrades slaughtered by the Germans during World War II, the Soviets were entitled to build a wall across Berlin or anywhere else they damned-well liked.

'With some filthy Jerry bitch, sir,' answered McNiel, and the Old Man sniggered maliciously.

'Is that so?'

'Yeah.'

'Let's hope for your sake, McNiel, that she wasn't *too* filthy. Don't expect time off to attend a V.D. clinic. You'll go in your own time... Right, two days' pay, and next time it's four, then eight... Believe me, McNiel, I can keep this up for longer than you.'

McNiel ambled away and the engine-room storekeeper appeared, spluttering and sneezing into a handkerchief. Camembert Robert, one of his hands, followed him dejectedly.

'Robert, sir,' he too croaked, pronouncing it 'Rober'. 'The t's silent, it's French... Rober.'

'What the hell's *wrong* with you, Stores?' the Old Man demanded suspiciously, at the same time deciding none of *his* men would have fancy, poncy names.

'Got flu, I fink, Cap'n.'

The Old Man grabbed his own handkerchief and slapped it

over his face. 'Then kindly leave at once,' he ordered, 'I don't want it.' Then, as an afterthought, 'should'v told that to the flaming bosun as well... might have it *already*!'

As he read the misdemeanours attributed to the present offender, his eyebrows rose in astonishment and he glared at him menacingly.

'You're on daywork, aren't you, Robert?' He ignored the French pronunciation and when Robert nodded, exploded. 'Then why haven't you *been* on bloody daywork? We've been here four days and this is the first time you've been back on board.'

'Bin in nick, Cap'n.'

'Wha...?'

'Bin in nick, Cap'n.'

'Wha... in *prison?*'

'Sir.'

'Why was I not informed?' he glowered at Angus McKenzie, whose burden it was to be present.

'Cos I wouldn't tell 'em who I was.'

'You wouldn't tell them who you was... er... were?'

'That's right, sir.'

'Why wouldn't you tell them who you were?'

'Cos then they'd 'ave known.'

'Known?'

'I mean... they'd 'ave found out.'

The Old Man's head dropped despairingly into his hands as he tiredly enquired, 'Found out what, you crazy bas...?'

'That they 'ad the wrong man.'

The Old Man raised his head again. 'I don't quite...'

'Well sir', began Robert, uneasily licking dry lips, 'I was up the Reeperbahn y'see, an' saw the chief mate. Drunk and disorderly 'e was, staggerin' about, singing an' exposing 'imself to a whore in a brothel winda.' He paused anxiously as the Old Man leapt to his feet, mouth working soundlessly, as if in a goldfish bowl. When he finally spoke, he did so loudly.

'DO YOU REALIZE WHAT YOU'RE SAYING?' he bellowed, incredulity in every syllable. 'ARE YOU OUT OF

YOUR FEEBLE MIND?' He spun to face Angus McKenzie who was now very much alert and watching with eager interest. 'IS THIS RATING OF YOURS INSANE?' The lips of the engineer barely managed to contain the smile of cruel anticipation.

'I swear it, sir,' insisted Robert, 'an' I 'aven't 'ad a drop.'

The Old Man regarded him as he would a dockside rat, then made hastily for his sleeping quarters, the mention of drink reminding him that the needed one, and fast. Tedward was guarding a case under the bed. Returning to his dayroom cum-office, he sat down heavily, head shaking in disbelief.

'You're *lying*!' he bawled. 'THIS IS THE MOST MONSTROUS, SLANDEROUS, EVIL ATTEMPT AT DECEIT I HAVE EVER ENCOUNTED, why... it's INEXCUSABLE...!'

'But sir...'

'A WORSE CONCOCTION OF FILTH AND INSOLENCE I HAVE YET TO...'

But Robert would not be silenced. He explained, quickly and concisely, how the lady, outraged by this violation of herself and public decency, had summoned the police poste-haste to arrest the man. The Old Man just stared, unseeingly, wondering if ears he'd always trusted were now beyond help.

'But why YOU?' he demanded.

'She'd said 'e was a Brit, an' when 'e scarpered like 'is arse was on fire... I was the only Brit there.' He stood, submissive under the Old Man's moody stare. The captain's brain worked feverishly.

It just couldn't be true... could it? Of course not. The highly respected Hercules Duff? Nonsense... Why the man was a pillar of propriety... the font of all morality... justifying the respect of... of... whom? Yes... dammit...! Whom? Not him or anyone he knew. Could then... this be correct? Were these deplorable deviations known to all but him? Had he been blind? His chief officer... His bible-punching prick of a first mate...? Just suppose... suppose, mind you... that these allegations were correct... and he... chose to take no action...

Christ! He needed another drink, but immediately.

Regaining his seat, still far from convinced, he scowled up at Robert suspiciously.

'If you were the innocent bystander in all this, why didn't you merely tell the truth... protest?'

'They might 'ave brought 'er aboard, sir, an' she might 'ave realized 'er mistake an'...'

'But why the mistake in the first place? Couldn't she identify...?'

'She 'adn't paid much attention to 'is face, sir.'

'Er... yes, yes, quite.' The Old Man rose and began pacing nervously. This was either true or the most diabolical... But would a rating *dare* lie to him about such...? He sat down again and said solemnly, 'Do you fully appreciate the gravity of these allegations?'

'I do, sir,' murmured Robert as the Old Man resumed his nervous pacing. 'I only wish it... wasn't, sir.' There was a degree of sympathy in his voice which discomforted the Old Man even further, and he paced through the door for another drink. Then, spinning on heels, he was back, asking with sudden inspiration.

'What about your I.D. card?'

'What difference would that make?'

'Oh.' The Old Man returned at once to the bottle. What should he do? Robert seemed sincere enough... but was he sincerely pulling the wool over his eyes? Should he have the whole sordid business out with Mr Duff there and then? No, no... for if this outrageous charge had any foundation, he didn't wish to tackle the man just yet, especially in the presence of a rating. But he would find a way, in his own good time, and gloat luxuriously as the filthy bastard squirmed and trembled his career down the toilet. So uplifting was the thought that he was almost prepared to leave the inquiry at that.

'Just let Jesus Christ get him out of this,' he sniggered, re-entering the day room.

'Sir?'

'Oh… nothing, nothing.' He stared pensively at Robert. Something still didn't ring true. 'But why,' he asked, 'didn't you just put them right?'

'And get the chief *imprisoned*, sir?' Robert was aghast. 'Who would *do* such a thing?' The Old Man was thinking "Me" for a start, but said nothing.

'And the scandal, sir,' he continued, 'just think of the scandal. Not just to the mate, sir, but the company, the ship… even,' a dramatic pause, '*yourself*.'

Paling, the Old Man licked parched lips, his scepticism ebbing fast. He'd long suspected something sinister lurking beneath all this ghastly, religious vulgarity but nothing remotely… His harassed attention focused once more on Robert, standing mutely before him, head bowed in loyal servitude, and his heart went out to him.

'Robert,' he whispered, voice thick with emotion.

'Sir?' came the almost inaudible reply. Robert was equally overcome.

'It would appear that we owe you a debt of gratitude.' Then to Angus McKenzie, 'Have you ever *seen* such loyalty… to the company… the ship… and *me*?'

The engineer smiled thinly.

'Just think, all that time in custody.'

Angus McKenzie *was* thinking. He must warn his second about this crafty bastard with more nerve than a bum tooth.

'Such exemplary conduct,' the Old Man went on, 'should not go unrewarded.'

'Oh, but sir…' protested Robert, 'there's no need… I mean… it was nothin'… really, sir…' His voice trailed away and the Old Man slapped his desk top delightedly.

'Just *listen* to the man,' he cried in wide-eyed admiration. 'Men like you Robert, are a credit to the Red Ensign.' He murmured something to Angus McKenzie who replied with a disinterested nod. 'Robert,' he declared, beaming paternally, 'in view of your recent selflessness I'm forgetting the time adrift, and the chief has agreed to give you the remainder of the day off. How's that?' He winked at the startled rating who gushed.

'Oh, thank y' sir, thank y' chief... I wasn't expecting...'

'But Robert,' the Old Man interrupted sternly, 'as I'm forgetting the past few days, I expect you to do likewise... understood? Not a solitary word must you utter to anyone.'

'Oh, I won't sir... I mean... a thing like this is best...'

'Exactly Robert... you may go.'

Barely had he reached the door when the Old Man called after him, beaming, 'Have a nice day,' and Robert fled back to the bar in which he'd spent the previous four days.

Grinning drunkenly into his tumbler, the Old Man wallowed in malicious thought. Oh, how stupid he'd been! It was so clear. The scotch that mysteriously vanished on every trip... and that bloody book of his... probably some literary filth in the dust jacket of the bible. Why, the bastard hadn't been praying at all, he'd just been too pissed to stand! The grin gave way to a sneer as vengeful images lurched through his confused mind. Suddenly exhausted, he groped his way to his daybed where he lay, fully clothed, and slept for two hours dreaming that he and Tedward were lashed to the drum of a winch, being subjected to every known humiliation by a hostile crew, mutinously led by Hercules Duff with his willy hanging out.

He was awoken by Chewsday, the second steward who doubled up as his tiger (personal steward), who informed him that the lunch he didn't want was being served. The cargo had almost finished being loaded and the vessel was due to leave for Antwerp late afternoon.

II

Mahoney was known as Phoney, partly because it rhymed and partly because of an obsession on which he spent much time, effort and money, untiringly but always in vain. Touts and pimps everywhere, knowing his quest, flocked to him with expensive information – the disclosures, however, purchased from gleeful foreign con-men, were always as phoney as himself.

It is not often that ladies who love ladies (he abhorred the word 'lesbian' – to him it failed to reflect the beauty involved, of shared love in a world largely bereft) are prepared to indulge their unique pleasures before a solitary male audience, even one willing to pay as handsomely as he. He never used the word and those who knew him didn't utter it within his earshot.

He had no desire to criticize or ridicule, merely to watch, and where was the harm in that? Explicit films left him cold for the professional performers were obviously insincere. He staunchly defended their rights but they, nevertheless, caused him inestimable masculine deflation. What could they do that he couldn't? What had they got that he hadn't? He longed to view the genuine, uncensored spectacle and learn where he was going wrong. It was irksome and sad that none of his shipmates shared his quest because, if he ever succeeded, to whom could he boast? It secretly upset him that he would never be the object of secret envy he secretly hoped to be.

He had been seated with the Snot Gobbler, in Anterp's Texas Bar, but the assistant steward had driven him away with his incessant opinionating.

'This bleedin' planet…' he proclaimed, snake-like tongue flicking out to lick the end of his nose.

'Not interested,' sighed Mahoney.

'…is a great, round caperhouse wot spins. Shakespeare 'ad it all wrong, y'know. It ain't no stage and us poor fuckers ain't no players. We're inmates, all committed by that eternal shrink in the sky and there's no way out, especially for phoney bastards like you.'

'Piss orf, will ya.'

'Even when y' dead there's no escape. They just move y' onto another ward – the treatment goes on…'

'Aw, for Chrisake…!'

'You,' continued the Gobbler, waving an admonishing finger, 'are a no-hoper… you're untreatable. If I 'ad my way, Phoney, you'd be fuckin' discharged from the whole institution. You're givin' us all a bad name.'

'Oh fuck!' sighed Mahoney, tiredly.

'I'm pleased about one thing, anyway, you're not Irish, in spite of your name. Tell ya wot!' exclaimed the Gobbler, inspired by a thought, 'I 'ear the mate spends 'alf 'is shore time in church prayin'. You should go along wi' 'im.'

'Why don't *you*?'

''Cos like you, 'e's a prod. I may not ''ave bin back to Ireland for donkey's years but ar'm still a catlick.'

'You're a cunt,' said Mahoney, getting to his feet and making for the door. His thoughts had wandered to the 'Zanzibar' with its select, exclusively female clientele, seated quietly in secluded booths. He would be there, he knew, though on many previous visits the atmosphere had left him in no doubt that his presence was decidedly unwelcome, as was any male custom.

'You're *dreamin'* man,' the Gobbler cried after him, invading his reverie. 'Wot about eh...? Ladies who love ladies?'

He slouched through the door, the shrill, mocking tones in his ears. 'Wod I tell ya? Wod I tell ya?' Mahoney wished the Gobbler would drop dead and move onto another ward.

Since leaving London a search had been underway for the bosun's cabin key.

At sea it didn't matter, doors were never locked anyway, but all knew that the only difference between the world's stevedores was their language of communication. Their language of thievery was universal. They would steal anything from a ship if it was not bolted down and at times, even then. His belongings, therefore, had been kept in the carpenter's cabin, next door. They had both stumbled aboard at midnight when they were approached on deck by Hercules Duff, looking quite triumphant and holding a key aloft. It was hurriedly placed in the bosun's outstretched hand as he tottered unsteadily with his shipmate who had acquired from somewhere a Caped Crusader's outfit which he wore. Looking quite perplexed, the mate had left at once.

Hardly had he arrived back in his quarters, when the bosun appeared with the key. 'Er... can't seem to get the lock movin' with this, chief... don't seem to fit...'

'Then get Batman to lock it for you,' he retorted, closing the door in his face.

Only then did he fully appreciate the spontaneity of his wit and felt an unaccustomed wave of rapture surge through his entire being. Had he really and truly said that? Get Batman to... His mind reeled joyfully as he heavily sank onto his bed, tittering uncontrollably, tears filling his eyes... Get Batman to... Oh, how he laughed. But that was *funny*, wasn't it? Yes, it was... *very* funny. He sat up, rocking back and forth, clutching his knees to his heaving chest in gratitude for the moment, unrefined pleasure streaming down his face as he savoured each heavenly convulsion... Get Batman to... He'd never said anything funny before.

In Danny's bar, an all-male preserve, the cook was busy in the retail of ladies underwear and toiletries. His short left leg did not hamper his progress at all but could be an encumbrance at sea, especially in rough weather. Being stood in the galley facing astern, when the ship rolled to starb'd, he'd find it imperative to hop round to face the bow to avoid keeling in the same direction. Then back to port she'd come with him repeating the manoeuvre.

His sales technique had been viewed with disinterest by Hambone Harrison, Suitcase Larson, Drunken Duncan and Downtown Daly. They were joined at their table by Black Eye McKay just as a disconsolate Mahoney entered and made for the bar.

'Where ya bin, Phoney?' McKay wanted to know, or rather didn't because he knew. 'Next door in the Zanzibar, I'll bet.' Mahoney merely shook a weary head.

The boys who were due on watch at midnight got up to leave for the ship and did so gratefully, for they had seen the Snot Gobbler enter. It wasn't long before he was getting up the noses of anyone who listened.

'Democracy?' he was saying. 'Britain is a *pretend*

democracy. The rulin' classes know it but it's in their interests, see? A true democracy wouldn't tolerate all these blood sucking aristocrats, breedin' like fuckin' rabbits at the tax-payers expense. Then they sit in the House of Unelected Wankers with bishops an' clapped out failures.

'Nobody's forcin' y' t'live there…'

'An' wot about the judges… the police chiefs… the mayors…? Elected? Not on y' fuckin' life. They're appointed by their cronies.'

'We got freedom o' speech.'

'Only providin' nobody listens to y'. If y' started drawin' crowds y'd be inside pronto on some charge like disturbin' the peace, *their* fuckin' peace of mind…'

* * *

Ordinarily the Old Man conducted himself as indisputable judge and jury with complete equanimity, but moments like this he anticipated with dread, for the offender was the cook. His profits in Danny's had exceeded all expectations and a justifiable celebration had ensued. The Old Man always harboured grave misgivings whenever he had to punish a cook. He was haunted by visions of the man subjecting the few meals he ate to the most revolting of meddlings such as rubbing his organ in the cabbage, spitting into the mashed potato and ejaculating into the chicken noodle soup.

Slumped at his desk, he stared dejectedly into space searching for a seemingly valid reason to dismiss all charges, whilst still satisfying Stanley Stone who had been obliged by the cook's absence to soil his hands with work. The knowledge that the chief steward required full and just penalty to be imposed weighed heavily, for *he* might try and poison him again. There was a quiet knock on the door which slowly opened to reveal the bent distraught figure of Stanley Stone.

'What is it now?' he snapped.

'Er… I'm afraid, sir,' he began dolefully, 'you can't log the cook this morning, sir.'

The Old Man's eyes widened in disbelief.

'Who says so?' he demanded. 'I can log whoever I damned-well please and that includes *you*, Mr Stone.'

The steward gave a sniff and the Old Man got to his feet for some indignant pacing. Can't log the cook? Who the hell would stop him? Of all the intolerable suggest... Hey! Wait a minute! What was that? Can't log the cook? Hiding his relief, he sat.

'Yes, I fully understand,' he said, nodding understandingly, 'he'll get what's coming to him eventually. You mark my words. The very next time he steps out of line I'll...'

'The next time you were talking about, sir, well it's already here.'

'The next time I was talking about is already here? What in blazes are you talking about?'

'The cook, sir... He's adrift again.'

'Damn and bloody...!' This was dreadful news, just when he thought... 'No sign of him at all?'

'No, sir,'

'Mmmmmmm.' The Old Man lapsed into thoughtful silence, broken only by the tap, tap of his pen on the desk top. This was an added complication he could have done without. This would mean double punishment for the cook which in turn could mean double defilement for... The tapping stopped abruptly and he looked up, a dim glimmer of inspiration deep within his eyes.

'Er...' he began, 'what makes you so certain that he *is* adrift?'

'It's plainly evident, sir... he can't be found.'

'That doesn't necessarily follow.'

'But he's not on board.'

'I sent him ashore.' The solution was clarifying in the Old Man's head now. 'I've only just remembered.'

'You gave him time off sir?' rejoined the steward in injured tone. 'But the catering crew are *my* affair. You could have at least informed me...' He found himself addressing an angrily waving finger.

'Yes, it *is* your bloody affair, but as master it is also mine!'

'Sir, I just meant…'

'Then don't.' He sank back wearily. 'Now… where was I…? Ah yes. I sent the cook ashore because I *wanted* the cook ashore. That is sufficient reason. Now get back to the galley and prepare the bloody lunch.'

'Er…' he shuffled, thoughtfully, 'will he be back in time to prepare dinner?'

'I doubt that very much,' the Old Man answered, grinning humourlessly.

'Oh.'

'Anyway…' he grumbled irritably, 'why all the fuss? You've got the second cook and baker to give you a hand.'

'I forgot to mention, sir… He's adrift as well.'

'Christ!' Horrid visions of him blowing his nose into cake mix flashed before him, and the old 'Ink Spots' number, 'Into each life some rain must fall but too much is falling in mine,' sang in his head. 'Er… then get the second steward to help you,' he directed, dismissing the man with an impatient wave as he made for his liquor cabinet, stopping abruptly as his mind's neon sign flashed *Danger!! This* bastard had tried to poison him *already.*

'Steward! Steward!' he bellowed. *'Come back!'*

In the doorway he appeared, hands clasped behind him as he sulkily surveyed his shoes.

'Er…' the Old Man began, in soothing tone, or at least one designed with that in mind, 'so you want to know why I sent the cook ashore?'

Stanley Stone shuffled again.

'Well,' continued the Old Man, 'you have the right to know. After all… it *is* your department.' He found smiling in an ingratiating manner impossible, but to appease, made a gallant attempt. 'Please be seated, Mr Stone…' Pouring himself a drink, he went on, inspired. 'I've heard so many compliments about the meals which you yourself prepared yesterday…' pausing, the oily flattery hitting its mark as the steward's head swelled visibly, '…that I decided to give you further opportunity. The cook will receive his just desserts for yesterday… have no fear… but as for today… that was *my* idea.' He signed dramatically, gazing at the deckhead above. 'A truly mouth-watering repast of inestimable worth, created by an expert, is such a rare treat afloat these days, it's surely worthy of abundant recognition.'

He stole a sly glance at the steward but needn't have been concerned. His eyes had glazed over and focused on nothing before him while his ears had absorbed, wrung dry and savoured every utterance. The former worry he had experienced on learning that he would have to take charge of the galley had been completely unfounded. He now knew he had coped, admirably… and even more than that.

'Well?' the Old Man enquired, plunging into his wistful, star be-decked fantasy. 'What do you think?' It was a full thirty seconds before he could reply.

'Wha…? Wha…? What do I *think* sir?' He sounded like a post-operative patient recovering from anaesthesia, and felt like one. 'I don't quite… er... know what to say… I'm really *thrilled…*'

'Everyone enjoyed it, tremendously.'

'Everyone?'

'Of course… Oh you should have heard them extolling… lip-smacking. It was a sight to behold…'

'Even the…' no surely this was expecting too much… 'the *ratings,* sir?'

'Even those hairy-arsed bastards lapped it up like starving hounds.'

So it was *true*. The heart of the steward floated enraptured. This was undeniable proof of his mastery. The ultimate accolade. He came proudly to his feet, yearning to be dismissed that he could fly to his quarters, there to give unrestrained vent to his bubbling elation.

'And now,' chuckled the Old Man, rubbing hands together, 'run along to the galley and begin. I can hardly wait for lunchtime. What delicacy can we anticipate today?'

'Well, I...'

'No, no,' he held up a restraining hand, 'don't tell me Mr Stone... Surprise me... Surprise us all.'

The steward floated away, transcendental, beyond the failing of mere mortals and no longer ill-disposed towards the cook whose misdemeanours had allowed his dormant talent to blossom in full blaze.

Alone again, the Old Man allowed himself a smile's glimmer at the indescribable conceit and naivety of the man. Not that he had lied. No one *had* complained about the meals: the officers didn't dare and the ratings, due to close proximity of the nearest bar, had not eaten. He had just poured himself a large celebratory measure when Chewsday appeared with a letter for him. Not a company business letter from head office or anywhere else but one marked 'Very Personal' – the first of such he had ever received in his entire life. He flopped down, staring in bewilderment at the headed first page. Had he contacted a Lonely Hearts Agency – before leaving London? In vain he attempted to recall and soon found himself staring into the eyes of Ms Beatrice Pouch from Burnham-on-Crouch, who stared back from the photo.

* * *

The chief steward required no assistance whatever. Jubilation had provided sufficient company as he confidently prepared the mid-day meal. He was even thankful for the absence of any interference in his art. The dish-of-the-day was to be Irish Stew and the Old Man's portion was to be larger than the rest and contain added exotic delicacies.

His captain and wonderfully perceptive master of the *Susan Snide* had asked for and would receive his surprise in munificence. Afloat upon clouds of vanity, bearing the tray on which reposed the silver tureen reserved for special occasions, and bubbling with schoolboy excitement, he reached the open door. His right eye shone, along with the left, in understandable expectation of liberal praise, when it was hit by a tightly screwed-up ball of paper which stung like hell. It closed instantly, throbbing in agony, but failed to adversely affect his grand entrance or diminish the gladness of his feather-like heart.

'Oh!' he cried, step faltering only slightly as he smiled doggedly. 'Jolly good shot, sir. Yes indeed!' Guided by his left eye, he advanced, lovingly setting down the tray on the desk before the Old Man. 'Here you are, sir,' he gushed, 'I just know you're going to enjoy this.'

'Huh?' The Old Man glared at him in sullen perplexity.

'It's your surprise sir,' he breathed, and with a servile flourish, lifted the lid. 'Mmmmmm,' he murmured dreamily. 'Doesn't that smell simply *divine*?' His left eye shone with pride as deserving shoulders prepared themselves for bountiful gratitude.

The Old Man's mood was filthy. His attempt to reply to the agency, acknowledging receipt of their communication and asking for an introduction to Ms Beatrice Pouch, was proving decidedly difficult. Concentration had deserted him. His morning's intake had cruelly robbed him of the ability to think clearly and the last thing he wanted was to make a fool of himself in writing, hence the scattered balls of paper.

He scowled at the stew and felt bilious – thick, steaming brown liquid, unappetizing gobs of greasy, fatty meat and fat-coated vegetables drifting on the surface like dunnage in a stagnant dock. He swallowed hard as the scalding combination of scotch and hydrochloric acid threatened to leap from his recoiling stomach.

'Close the other eye and turn around,' he ordered. The scowl had become a leer and his narrowing eyes glinted like steel at the beaming steward.

'Around, sir?'

'Yes. I now have a surprise for *you*.' And even the disabled eye widened in happy anticipation as hands were clasped behind him.

'A *surprise*... for ME?' he cried, unable to contain his joy. 'Oh, but sir... thank you... you shouldn't have... I mean...

I've quite enjoyed the cooking... really I have.'

He spun around. 'Oh sir,' he squealed, 'I adore surprises... and... coming from you...'

From him it came. The up-turned tureen enveloped his head and he frantically charged for where he imagined the doorway to be. Muffled screams could be heard from his stewing head. Grinning drunkenly, the Old Man watched him hit the bulkhead twice before discovering the aperture, the now empty receptacle rattling around his skull.

Alone again, he gently eased his heavy, troubled head onto the desk top where he slept uneasily. He and Tedward were being lashed to the drum of a winch, to suffer every humiliation known to man from a hostile crew being egged on by Stanley Stone. He awoke drenched in cold sweat, thankful at least that they were leaving for Le Havre on the morrow, to load the last of the cargo before heading out for open sea.

Slow Ahead

The young, pre-war Stanley Stone had, with admirable dedication, served for a year on his first ship, the ill-fated *Rose Snide*, before becoming aware of the vivacious Vyvyn K, and then, purely by chance. He'd been despatched to head office on an errand. The ambitiously arrogant assistant steward was instantly captivated by the aloofness encountered and it was love at first sight.

Fate, he reasoned, had pre-ordained their being in the same room together. Never had he been this close to such class and the off-handedness with which he'd been dealt sailed serenely over his head, subjugating not, the mutual attraction he felt was thick in the air. This was confirmed several months later by his promotion to the *Lady Snide* as her second steward. He'd heard, of course, that Vyvyn K had specific sexual preferences (don't many of us?), whereas he had no detectable leanings one way or the other. Still, for the advancement he craved, he'd be more than prepared to give it his best shot.

This promotion could not have been better timed – a lifesaver, for shortly after this happy acquaintance, the *Rose* had met with her inglorious end. So, through Vyvyn K, who treated the old values with the same contempt as he, his life was now charmed, great heights to attain... the prestigious post of catering superintendent perhaps... or even a directorship. Today a second steward... but tomorrow...?

At start of war, Sir Reg had zealously immersed himself in his newly acquired venture of immeasurable lucrativity, having astutely harnessed an American wife and yet more irons for the fire – shooting irons. Still, mused Stanley sadly, it was war, and the subsequent reduction of staff at head office had obviously rendered Whippit-Snide the younger, far too engrossed to reply to his innumerable, grovelling letters.

When hostilities ended and still no word came, the fretting began in earnest, his depression being aggravated by the particularly hurtful rumour linking the heir apparent with some upstart second mate of the *Anne Snide*.

This cloud over his future disturbed him constantly until his promotion to chief steward of the *Daisy*, and the opportunity to establish foreign markets for the disposal of ship's stores, the administration of which now juicily fell to him on each ship he served. With no hope now of his directorship and a diminishing one in the lesser position of catering superintendent, his pockets needed lining by more drastic means. Early retirement had been his initial aim but greed kept getting in the way for, as chief steward, embezzlement was a duty and not to fulfil it to the highest level would be downright criminal.

After this he spent several highly profitable years on the *Sarah*, aided by a master who assumed him to be as honest as himself. He made no demands on his time and left him largely to his own devices. His grief, therefore, was profound when Captain Arbuckle fell dead on deck in Montevideo whilst yarning with chief engineer, Angus McKenzie.

'This one'll kill ya, Bill,' Angus had said, and recounted a bizarre spectacle, witnessed years before through an open door aboard the *Anne Snide*, ' …actually talking to a bloody *teddy bear*, he was…'

His audience had thrown back his head to begin the guffaw from which he never recovered.

It had fallen to Angus to receive and welcome the new captain at the airport the following week and he'd gasped audibly upon recognition of the approaching figure. Eyes momentarily closed, head wearily shook before he reluctantly stepped towards him.

'Cap'n?' he ventured, forcing politeness, and the Old Man stopped, ignoring the proffered hand.

'Mmmmmph,' he grunted, squinting with distaste at the face before him, a face he sourly recalled as belonging to some gladly half-forgotten engineer. 'And you're the chief engineer, I suppose?' He looked around. 'Where's the chief officer?'

'He's back on...'

'Never mind, never mind,' he glanced impatiently at his watch. This was not what he had expected. 'And the chief steward...?'

'He's still on...'

'Never mind, never mind,' came the dismissive growl. This was not entirely befitting... unworthy of his new rank. Even the brass band was absent. Huffily he strode away, followed by Angus McKenzie and a porter pushing a luggage trolley.

What the hell was *happening* here? A thought struck him suddenly and he stopped, obliging Angus and the porter to do likewise. 'The chief steward,' he asked thoughtfully, 'what's his name?'

'Er... Stone.'

'Stone?' His eyes darkened with suspicion.

'Yeah.'

'*Stanley* Stone?'

'Ah believe so... yeah... I dinna tak much notice of...'

'That's very astute of you, Mr... er...'

'McKenzie... Angus McKenzie.'

'Mmmmmmm.' He resumed his walk for several paces before once more stopping. 'Er...,' he began, to McKenzie's annoyance, '...just how did old Arbuckle die...? Any signs of sickness... diarrhoea... before the end?'

'No,' replied the dour Scot, shaking his head. 'Ah'd 'ave known. We were good friends.'

'Mmmmmm.' They walked on. 'Then how did he die?'

The engineer snapped his fingers dramatically. 'Just like that.'

'Just like tha... tha... that?' repeated the Old Man, snapping his fingers at the third attempt.

'Aye,' drawled Angus sadly. 'He was laughin', y'see, an'...'

'WHAT?' The Old Man stopped so suddenly that the

porter had to take evasive action to avoid running into him with the trolley.

'Like ah said… He was laughin'.'

'But… surely… you… don't mean… he… actually… er… *died*… laughing?'

'Ah'm afraid so,' came the sorrowful reply.

'And… er… were you present at the time?'

'Yeah.'

'And at what,' called the Old Man over his shoulder, having resumed the walk, '…was he laughing?'

He got his answer through a thin smile. 'Oh… just some old yarn.' In silence they continued for a while, then the Old Man stopped once more, turning to face the engineer, eyes round with fear.

'Mr. McKenzie,' he said, face paling.

'What?'

'Remember never to tell it to *me*… okay?'

He had retained command of the *Sarah* until his present posting, the *Susan*. This made him the company's commodore master. Upon first receiving notification he had hoped to be removed as far away as possible from the deplorable Stanley Stone and provide the *Susan's* new chief engineer with the shock of his life – a pleasant thought.

* * *

The *Sarah* had been well into her final voyage before anyone found out it *was* her final voyage. Stanley Stone had heard it first and came howling to the Old Man from the radio room where he'd been chatting to the sparks.

'Oh, sir, sir,' he wailed, wringing his hands in woe as his misted eyes tried to focus on the Old Man's office carpet, on which the Old Man lay. 'Appalling news, sir. Appalling news.'

'Huh? Who said that?' came the muffled response through carpet fibres.

'It's… me, sir,' the steward whined, as the Old Man raised his head and turned over with a gasping struggle.

'Oh,' he yawned, squinting distastefully at the intruder. 'Wha…? Applauding Jews?'

'Appalling *news*, sir. *Terribly* appalling news.'

With the long drawn-out sigh of the unjustly damned, the Old Man sat up, belched loudly and rested back on his hands. He was instantly aware of intestinal sensation which eased the moment he tunefully broke wind.

'Well… out with it,' he snapped. 'And it had better be bloody appalling.'

'It's the *Sarah*, sir…'

'What about her?'

'She's been *sold*.'

'To Israel?'

'Gr…Greece, sir.' The steward's shoulders heaved spasmodically. It was a black day… all his nurtured markets under threat once more. After looking thoughtful for a while, the Old Man attempted to wave a reproving finger but found his balance being lost so he abandoned the idea.

'*You're lying.*'

'I… wish… I was… sir.'

'Since when has Greece been a Jewish nation?'

'Oh sir… please try and understand,' he pleaded. 'Our ship has been sold from under us… *sold*.'

'OUR *ship*? She's *my* bloody ship and if she's been sold, I'll be assigned another… *our* bloody ship, indeed.' He eased himself back, reclining in reflection. 'I can't understand the Jews buying this old crate. I'll bet the Greeks have bought her for scrap.'

'Oh, no, sir…' whispered the steward, wearily, 'the Israelis…'

'Greeks.'

'Israelis, sir.'

'The *Greeks, dammit!*' he yelled, sitting up as the sparks entered to inform him of the transaction. The Old Man shot a triumphant glance at Stanley Stone, told him to dry his eyes and get out.

'There was another wire, sir,' offered the sparks, 'for Mr

McKenzie…' Prompting eyebrows shot up. 'He's been promoted, sir… to the flagship, the *Susan.*'

'Has he now?' remarked the Old Man dryly, and lapsed into moody speculation.

Reclining once more his eyes mirrored his thought. Odds and bloody Bods. How in hell did *he*…? But the *Susan*, of all ships… this would make him commodore chief engineer! Oh… it was *too* much… the man was conceited enough *already*. The Old Man had no say in the appointment of engineers, but dammit all…! He was an uncouth reprobate, a pillock of society, totally unsuited to such social status… Why, he'd never even been suspected of having an influential relationship with… His wretched contemplations were interrupted by a jubilant Angus McKenzie who skipped in, waving his wire.

'See *me*,' he bubbled. 'See *ME!*' eyes darting about, missing the recumbent figure on the carpet over which he went sprawling.

'Ah HAH!' he exclaimed, getting up and victoriously brandishing the message. 'See THIS! It's mah passport from *you*, ye *bastard*!' His unbridled celebrations made the Old Man wince inside. 'What d'ye propose t' dae aboot *that?*'

'What do I propose to do…? What *can* I do?'

'Exactly! Exactly!' cackled the engineer. 'There's bugger all y'*can* do. See ME! See ME!'

He began leaping over the Old Man's prostrate figure, first one way, then the other, holding the wire aloft like a battle standard. *'Ability! Ability!'* he raved. *'That's how ah got this post! AH'M no yes man or dicky licker! See ME! See ME! Why… ah'v never even been suspected of having an influential relationship wi…!'*

'GET OUT! YOU'RE GIVING ME A BLOODY HEADACHE!'

'See ME! See ME! There's only one way ah can go now!' he ranted. *'An' ye know what THAT IS… Bix… ye bastard?'*

The Old Man did not reply, having a finger stuck firmly in each ear as he watched the hurdling engineer.

'*Right slap bang into the shore superintendent's office…
THAT'S where… Right slap bang…!*' Becoming bored with
leaping he switched to hopping by way of diversion and landed
a heel in the Old Man's crotch.

'AHHHHHHEEEEEE!'

'See ME! See ME!' sang the happy Angus, skipping out
through the door.

Stanley Stone was inconsolable. Valuable and established
contacts with South American ship's chandlers who were as
crooked as himself were now on the brink; harmonious
associations which had taken years of dedication were now to
be lost. The dear *Sarah*, bless her charitable heart, had been his
most profitable vehicle, smiling generously on his wheelings
and dealings. What brutal retribution did the gods demand?
How could they treat him thus? It made a mockery of
Christianity, the 'Judgement' should not precede death. At this
rate he'd have nothing to answer for.

'Oh *Sarah*,' he moaned. 'What have they done to us?'

'See ME! See ME!' cried the happy engineer, skipping in.
'Ah'm goin' tae the *Susan!*'

'That's… er… nice,' came the hardly audible reply from
the steward who already knew. He raised his damp face from a
sodden towel. 'Congratulations.'

'NICE!' retorted the incredulous Scot. 'NICE! It's more
than bloody nice! *YOU* won't be there, ye weepin', wailin'
bastard!' and out he skipped again.

* * *

Angus McKenzie had deemed it wise to forgo his leave
entitlement. Apart from not caring where he spent it, for he had
no family and like many seafarers of many years standing,
he'd lost contact with what friends he ever had. Shipmates
were regarded as merely Board of Trade acquaintances, to be
suffered. He had no faith whatever in those poncey Sassenachs
in Leadenhall Street either. They might even reconsider his
elevation to the flagship. So, leaving the *Sarah* at her Tilbury

berth, he travelled overnight to the South Shields dry dock where the *Susan* was undergoing her annual survey.

Unlike many of his countrymen, his favourite booze was gin and he had ensured his arrival with a plentiful supply on which he started within minutes of his boarding. The exquisite prospect of life without the Old Man enhanced its flavour to equal nectar from some angelic distillery and a resolution to partake of, only moderately, quickly dissolved. Soon he was serenading and praising his brilliance as a lyricist. To the tune of 'I belong to Glasgow', he sang –

'Ah'm the commodore chief. Ah'm the commodore,
Nae one can call me a mere engineer anymore,
If Bix, the bastard were here right now,
The disgustin' old drunken slob.
Ah'd say get ashore, ye old son of a whore,
There's not even a greaser's job.'

The raucous self-appreciation filled his accommodation to be interrupted by a knock on the door, which opened.

'Oh, hello chief!' exclaimed the caller. 'I saw you come aboard and thought I'd take this opportunity to introduce myself.'

'That's a sharp pair o' eyes ye have there laddie,' came the slurred reply.'Y' know... ah should'na wonder if you're in navigatin'.'

'First mate, chief,' said the visitor, coming forward to shake his hand. 'Hercules Duff is the name... please call me... er Hercules. I've only recently been assigned to the vessel myself.'

'Very well, Hercules,' he nodded drunkenly, 'Ah'm Angus McKenzie... please call me commodore... Here... have a drink.'

'Oh, no thank you, I never touch it.'

'Is that...' there was incredulity in the engineer's voice, '...a fact?' He'd never before come face to face with a teetotaller.

'Yes,' came the reply. 'And there's a fire in the engine-room.'

'A fire in the engine room? Have ye called oot the brigade?'

'No need, apparently. The shoreside fitters assure me it is only of minor proportion... drips from a welding rod caught some lagging. They've probably extinguished it by now.'

'The brigade shoulda still bin called.'

'Well, there's a ship-to-shore phone in here.'

'Is there?' Dazedly he looked around him.

'Yes, so, if you wish to call out the brigade... to be on the safe side... The only other ship-to-shore phone is in the captain's quarters, which are locked. I don't have a key.'

'Where is he?'

'We don't have one at the moment. He was appointed to the marine superintendent's office. His replacement will arrive soon.'

'Mmmmmmmmm,' Angus murmured, deep in thought. 'Have ye any idea who?'

'Oh,' came the shrugged response, 'whoever is appointed to the new commodore master's post.'

At that Angus McKenzie exploded.

'*The bastards!*' He viciously punched the open palm of a hand as the startled mate backed uneasily towards the door. '*Oh the rotten, connivin' bastards! Ah might 'ave known they wouldna' let me be the only one! LOWDOWN BASTARDS!*'

'Er...' began the mate uneasily, '...about the fire, chief?'

'Huh?'

'The fire, chief.'

'Fire chief...? Fire chief...? Is that some new rank? Nobody said ah'd be sailin' wi' a fire chief? Is *he* a fuckin' commodore as well?'

'No, no. You misunderstand. There *is* no 'fire chief'.'

'Then why should ah call oot the brigade?' He returned to his gin, leaving the bemused Hercules Duff to wander ashore for evensong and quietly pray for a tolerant, understanding master as it was obvious that the chief engineer was a few cards short of a full deck.

* * *

When Stanley Stone had sadly left the sold *Sarah Snide* at Tilbury, he had made for the Anchor House at Canning Town where he booked a room to await his new appointment, unaware that the flagship's steward was in Newcastle Infirmary undergoing major surgery to remove his money belt; seafaring career over, the shock was to prove too great. His subsequent promotion, therefore, was more to do with his availability than what he'd assumed – that Vyvyn K, wracked with guilt at his abandonment, had used his influence in that direction.

Thus did he become chief steward of the *Susan*; the most prestigious steward of the Line. Never again would he be insulted, undervalued, ridiculed, patronized or metaphorically trodden on. He intended to inform, in no uncertain terms, the commodore master, of his close affiliation with the company's second-in-control. The crème-de-la-crème of stewards, and wouldn't Mr McKenzie be surprised.

Mr McKenzie *was* surprised. He and Hercules Duff, the only two officers working-by the dry docked vessel, were having lunch in the saloon. He had just forked a particularly hot portion of potato into his mouth when he happened to notice the familiar figure passing by a window outside on the companion-way. The potato slid down whole.

'Stone!' he choked, face contorting as he kneaded his burning throat. Mr Duff was equally surprised but more than willing to join in the game.

'Er... Gall stone?' he ventured hopefully.

'Stone! Stone!' gasped Angus, collapsing across the table, face contorting and turning blue. The mate scratched his chin. This was a toughie and no mistake... Wait 'til it was *his* turn.

'Stone... er... Henge?' he asked, as the newly appointed *chief* chief steward came to the rescue. He had waited years to make good use of his basic First Aid knowledge, and also to kick Angus McKenzie up the arse, which is how he dislodged the offending potato.

II

Beatrice Pouch had long since left Burnham-on-Crouch, occupying a bed-sit in Tooting, close to her widowed father. The not unexpected knock on her door obliged her to quickly return to the envelope, the letter she had been engrossed in with considerable eagerness. The separate photo she stuffed into her bra, catching her breath, for the print was cold against her breast.

She was twenty-eight, single and had been an ardent feminist since before the term existed. Not one of Mahoney's ladies who loved ladies, she felt she had little in common with the average female. She disliked what she took to be their idiotic conversation, their ready tolerance of hardship and their lack of personal motivation and she sought out the company of men with whom she felt a close affinity. She played a mean hand of poker and was competent both on the snooker table and the dartboard. She could match them pint for pint, swear foully, argue her corner forcefully, tell the filthiest of jokes, fart like the clappers and fight and pee accurately from a standing position. She had enjoyed several lovers, some of whom still bore the scars. Today, however, her countenance was sanguineness personified.

'Enter,' she called happily, and her community nurse, Ivy, breezed in, as was her custom, to administer medication from her black bag and generally monitor progress since her last discharge from in-patient care. For Beatrice had a slight relating problem which, she quite reasonably argued, was not entirely of her own making. It was not her fault that there were so many obnoxious individuals out there so deserving of physical assault.

'And how are we today, then?' enquired Ivy, settling into a chair like a quizzical mother hen.

'Me?' laughed Beatrice, eyes aglow. She spoke as if reborn. 'I'm fine… *really*. I *am* smashing, in fact.' The concern at this news was evident in Ivy's eyes. When Beatrice felt smashing, it was usually a prelude to something or someone being smashed.

'Mmmmm,' came the doubtful response, and Beatrice continued.

'Honestly... I feel great, *super*... I really do.'

Ivy viewed her with professional curiosity. She had never known Beatrice feeling *this* good, but could not be expected to know. After years of hoping to land a wealthy man and thus be able to travel the world, she'd discovered the next best thing – a ship's captain on an agency's books and he'd expressed interest in *her*.

'Have you been getting out and about much lately?' Ivy enquired.

'Oh... not much,' pouted Beatrice, who didn't want to give the game away, and beside, she was running out of disguises. So well was she known to the local constabulary, they would often pick her up on sight and deposit her at Tooting Bec Hospital.

'So you're not... er... seeing anyone at the moment?'

'No, just Sam, from time to time.'

'Sam?'

'New chap. Just moved in a couple of weeks back, across the hall.'

'Is it serious?' she asked, and Beatrice laughed out loud.

'No,' she stretched languidly, face down on the sofa, 'and it's not going to be. I'm saving myself.'

'Good,' said a relieved Ivy, more concerned about this Sam's well-being than any virtue left in her patient.

'Well,' said a resigned Beatrice, 'let's get it over with.' She duly hitched up her skirt and pulled down her knickers. The intra-muscular injection to reduce the tension she far from felt just then, plunged into the upper and outer quadrant of her right buttock.

Ivy was worriedly concerned. Beatrice was much too happy. She made a mental note to inform the consultant psychiatrist without delay. These were disturbing developments for now there was this fellow Sam and he could wind up very ill, very ill indeed… just like the vicar.

* * *

And very ill indeed was the vicar. In fact, he was dying and you can't get more ill than that. Earlier suspicions of carcinoma had sadly been confirmed and was by now spreading throughout his failing frame. He had been terrifyingly aware of this for some time having arrived at the conclusion without medical assistance, concealing his fear beneath clerical veneer – it just wouldn't do to flaunt it.

He had ceased his daily ritualistic duties on the advice of his undertaker and found that even prayer was becoming fatiguing. A relief vicar had been invoked who duly took over the parish's dwindling band of affluent devotees.

During this bedridden, precious, last few days, the cuckolded clergyman had allowed his mind free rein. It was now too late for mental restraint. Surely the world that awaited him would forgive a few, harmless excursions into sin after a lifetime of unquestioning dedication. Anyway, such ponderings diverted him from the unpleasant present.

I mean… suppose there *was* no God… or heaven… or after life… merely oblivion. Had his unique existence been squandered in religious, claustrophobic gloom, extolling the doctrines of imaginative mythologists? If so, there was, he supposed, some comfort to be gleaned from the fact that none would ever know what a blithering sucker he'd been. All these wasted years instead of doing what comes naturally… kinky sex, booze and drugs.

Yet another source of disquiet was that the evolutionary theories were now being regarded as historical *fact.* Still, he reasoned, mind-crippled humanity would always need support, particularly of the abstract variety, which could never be either proven or disproven. Even if it were… even if science were to threaten religious beliefs… would these audacious boffins accept responsibility for their discoveries… for kicking away the crutches of disabled mankind? He thought not. Besides it was all academic anyway, for the evidence of God living is all around us, from the humble earthworm to the American dollar on which it clearly states 'In God We Trust'. I mean... they wouldn't have *done* that, *would* they?

Late in the day it was for regrets; he still wished he had travelled more, seen for himself the result of one week's labour. He had ventured abroad only once, a honeymoon trip a decade ago, an idyllic cruise to the Canary Islands, at least, that's how it had begun. Then came the outrageous plot to trick him into working his passage.

'Er... why should the captain wish to see me?' he had enquired of the uniformed youngster who had borne the news.

'I'm sorry sir, I don't know.'

'Why don't you know?'

'Well... I...' the boy had not expected this and squirmed with discomfort. The vicar, a curate then, had frowned and bit his lower lip in contemplation.

'Have I...' he asked, '...done something wrong?'

'I really don't know sir,' the apologetic lad replied.

'Didn't he tell you?

At this the boy laughed nervously. A master does not take a minion to underlings into his confidence. Besides which, the captain's orders had been given to him by a lesser mortal.

'No, sir,' came the meek reply. He was being observed through narrowing eyes.

'How many passengers are aboard this ship?'

'About six hundred.'

'Six hundred... and he sends for *me*?'

'I just don't know why, sir.'

'Why do you keep *saying* that? To prevent *me* from knowing?'

In the event, the captain had been enormously relieved to find an ordained minister among his passengers. The Sunday morning service he found a loathsome chore and felt incapable of preaching the divine Christian word in a believable manner. He found faith of the religious variety quite questionable. The more far-fetched the belief, the more faith was needed to believe it. So the more filled with faith one was, then the more unconvincing the belief. To him it was as simple as that. Still, he had to admit, there were far more questionable sky-hooks on which to hang your hat.

'Ah!' he exclaimed heartily, beaming, 'come in Reverend, come it... pull up a pew. Ha ha ha.'

The response was uncompromising. 'Thank you, but I prefer to stand.'

'Suit yourself, Reverend, suit yourself. I'll come straight to the point. Y'see, I myself conduct the Sunday morning service in the passenger lounge... but now... with *you* on board... I mean... well... each to his own, eh?'

'Do I understand you correctly, captain?' the curate asked, frowning with displeasure. 'You expect me to...'

The captain seemed puzzled for a moment, then comprehension dawned.

'Oh, I see! No... the congregation will comprise only passengers with a few senior officers thrown in for show. I assure you, no rating will be present.' He winked. 'There'll be quite a gathering... larger than you'll find ashore, even at Christmas, with hardly a black hearted atheist among 'em.' He winked again. 'A captive audience. What d'you say?'

'Well...' drawled the ungrateful cleric, after an uncomfortable, protracted silence. 'Did you take a honeymoon cruise, Captain?'

'What? You wouldn't catch me *paying* to go to sea. Why... that would be like...'

'Forgive me, but if you *had*, would you have wished to involve yourself in sailing the ship?'

'Why... of course not, I...'

'You would wish to forget your responsibilities for the duration... am I right?'

'Well... yes... I suppose so,' he grudgingly admitted, but...'

'And I, Captain, wish to forget mine. I even *married* in a registry office to avoid reference to God, Jesus, The Holy Ghost, the Holy Spirit, Uncle Tom Cobbleigh and all.

Now, if you'll excuse me, my bride awaits.' Turning swiftly on his heels, he strode out, leaving the master mariner open-mouthed.

'Jesus H Christ!' he lamented to himself, little wonder the world was full of black- hearted atheists when all an ordained minister of the church was interested in on his honeymoon was fanny... The dirty bastard.

* * *

The vicar's eyes opened tiredly, then grew round with concern. His wife, the male nurse and his housekeeper were grouped around his bed, being led in prayer by the replacement vicar, who was the first to notice they were being fearfully observed.

'W...w...what the...?' the patient managed, 'in the name of...?' his feeble voice fading as eyes closed wearily. He had been comatose and had not been expected to recover.

Shuffling with acute embarrassment, the young clergyman grinned sheepishly and began to apologise.

'Er... well. You see, Daniel... I'm afraid I'm... er... unfamiliar with all this and thought... as you were sleeping...' The sick man's relief was evident. He'd only been asleep. This whole procedure was just a dummy run... Thank fuck for that.

'Ah well, Daniel...' he said in brisk joviality, 'I can't stand here all day... I have work to do. I'll say goodbye, see ya later then.' Which he did, encased in pine.

When the sombre group dispersed, the nurse returned to read the newspapers to him. Sadly dwelling on his celestial reception, the vicar suddenly pricked up his ears, for the nurse, himself an inveterate gambler, was reading the racing section and unwittingly generating his patient's last surge of interest.

The horses were called 'Pearly Gates', 'Holy Moses', 'Arch Angel', and 'St David'. On a wild and sinful impulse, he sent the nurse to place some heavy betting and expired with a smile on his grey face. Now so rich he would never again have to rely on grudging, ecclesiastical hand-outs.

The nurse quit his job immediately and became a missionary, having placed the same bets.

Half Ahead

When the *Susan Snide* entered Biscay, the Old Man had not fully recovered from a state of stuporous catatonia. Hercules Duff was in command and, encouraged by meteorological reports, had confidently prayed for clement weather conditions. Within hours she was in the grip of a merciless tempest which had appeared from nowhere.

Bulkheads groaned and creaked as she nose-dived into each approaching trough, her screw spinning crazily as her lifting stern cleared the wind-lashed seas.

Directly above, in the crew's accommodation, men clung for support to anything in the violent heaving and shaking. Then the bow, water cascading from every quarter, laboriously rose towards the stars while the stern plunged and pummelled, thrashing once more into the foaming turmoil, the submerging screw thumping and threshing its way down beneath the churning surface. Pens, matchboxes, ashtrays, books and timepieces flew through the air as those attempting to sleep tied themselves down with blankets to avoid being tossed, like unwanted toys from a petulant pram, to where chairs tumbled and rattled at will.

In the mess and galley, cutlery clattered, plates smashed, jars and bottles lay in shattered heaps of colour and, throughout the pandemonium, the steering gear whined its shrill, futile objection.

At the onset of the approaching storm, the chippie had charged around the vessel, securing storm doors and porthole deadlights – those within the hull being in particular danger of turning the ship into a colander if smashed. Up in the lurching, pendulous wheelhouse, Oddball McCall was at the helm, striving to maintain somewhere near the set course whilst, at the same time, determinedly preventing the struggling vessel from being overwhelmed and swamped by the violent conditions. He glanced at the wheelhouse clock. Ten minutes to go then before his relief in the shape of Hard Nut Neilson. They'd enjoyed some wild times together over the years but he'd never known anything as wild as Neilson's Le Havre episode.

* * *

'Yes, Mr Duff?' the Old Man had enquired, glancing up from his desk to where the mate stood fidgeting before him. He had ordered that the large timber stall in which was a valuable breeding bull, bound from Le Havre to Mombasa, be made secure in the comparative shelter of the mid-ship housing on the aft'deck.

'Well, sir,' he began uneasily, 'we've... er... had a spot of... er... bother.'

'Bother?'

'One of the deckhands... Neilson...' his voice trailed away.

It had transpired that the rating in question had returned aboard somewhat the worse for drink and upon seeing the bull, had removed his red shirt to drape it, cape-like over his arm – a marlin spike hidden in his hand beneath. He had then attempted to release the bull for some deck sport.

'It seemed he wanted to do-a-matador,' the mate explained.

'WHAT?' The Old Man shot to his feet. 'YOU MEAN I'VE GOT A FRIGGING BULL CHARGING AROUND?'

'No, no... he was prevented from...'

'Thank Christ for that!' he said, sinking back into his chair and not noticing the wince of disgust on Mr Duff's face at his blasphemy. 'How is he now?' he asked.

'Neilson or the bull, sir?'

The Old Man's head shook with exasperation. Was he surrounded by incompetents? 'TO HELL WITH NEILSON!'

he bellowed. 'HOW'S THE BLOODY BULL?'

'Oh… he'll survive. No harm done… Not on *that* score… anyway'

'What then?'

'Well… er…' His hesitancy was not unfounded and it took a few moments before he gathered the courage. The incident had been witnessed by the owner of the beast who, having not yet received payment for the animal, had decided that the *Susan Snide* would not carry it after all.

'Tell that bastard Neilson,' fumed the Old Man, 'that's he's been logged one month's pay.'

* * *

The Old Man was very partial to a drop of cognac, good French cognac in particular. He stood drooling on the wing of the bridge as several hundred tons of the stuff were loaded. Unable to face the spectacle any longer, he descended to the main deck level, biting thoughtfully on his lower lip. Thorndyke Camp and Cornelius Tinkler, second and third mates respectively, were overseeing the operation.

'Ah, Mr Camp!' he greeted amiably. The second mate spun around in some alarm. Rarely did the Old Man appear down here and seldom was he amiable.

'Sir?'

'Has anyone checked the contents of the brandy cases?'

The second officer's brow furrowed anxiously and he glanced hopefully toward his colleague for support, who offered none.

'I don't quite understand, sir,' he smiled uneasily. 'For a moment I thought you asked if anyone had checked the contents of the brandy cases.'

'I did.'

Thorndyke Camp ran puzzled fingers through his hair. What an odd question.

Why would anyone wish to check inside the brandy cases? He stared blankly at the Old Man, repeating in puzzlement…

'Has anyone checked the contents of the brandy cases sir?'

The Old Man ran puzzled fingers through *his* hair. 'Mmmm... an excellent suggestion Mr Camp,' he replied, 'yes... very astute.'

He approached Big Deal McNiel and Downtown Daley, who were none too busily chipping old encrusted paint from handrails. At his appearance, their hammers became accelerated blurs in the air.

'All right, you two! All right!' he yelled above the din, and they turned to face him.

'Er... wot's wrong, sir?' Daley enquired nervously. The news of Neilson having to work without pay had already adversely affected crew morale.

'I'm not sure,' said the Old Man guardingly, 'but I can't take any chances. I want you both to go down the hatch and fetch up a case of brandy for inspection. I am concerned that this method may be being employed to smuggle guns into Africa. Deposit it in my office.'

Gleefully they made off, rubbing hands and licking lips as they did so. 'And be quick about it!' he called after them, doing the same.

I mean... he *had* to give them *some* sort of explanation, hadn't *he*? Otherwise the whole damn crew would be suspecting him of broaching cargo for his personal use. He couldn't allow that. There was no telling *where* it might lead. It might enter their blasted thick skulls to do likewise. No... that would never do.

* * *

Through the mighty tossing seas she plunged – her progress almost nil even though the engine was at Full Ahead. She banged and clanged, shuddering and shaking like a wet dog, lost for protracted seconds in valleys of wrath, mastheads flapping in pathetic vulnerability, then to rise, as if gasping for breath, as spray ran down the inside of her funnel, belching smoke and steam – then once more to plunge in another corkscrew dive, with battened-down hope.

Down below in the engine-room, the conditions proclaimed their turbulent presence as punishingly as elsewhere. Tools and equipment from maintenance work inadvertently left on boiler tops, in hidden recesses and countless nooks and crannies, were being dislodged. The vessel's oscillations sent metal paraphernalia, including discarded nuts and bolts, raining down to where the engineer, donkeyman and fireman, slithered and slipped on oily deck plates as it bounced from pipes and catwalks. The engine roared and groaned, then raced crazily as the screw broke surface from her swirling wake, only to remonstrate discordantly when forced to take up the strain once more.

For what seemed eternity, they battled Biscay, by which time the cook had almost worn a hole in the galley deck, rotating on one leg in an effort to remain upright. Thence for the Gibraltar Straits as the weather improved by the hour. The placid blue Mediterranean awaited her arrival at a steady nine knots.

'What the...?' muttered Mahoney, entering the mess, rubbing sleep from his eyes ready for his watch. The object of his query lay upon a table.

'Never seen a cat afore, Phoney?' asked One Way Rogers, who had faintly heard a feeble meow coming from under a winch, where presumably it had survived the maelstrom.

'Is that wot it is?' Mahoney studied it from a distance, then asked, puzzled. 'Where the fuck did it come from?' I've seen plenty o' migratin' birds land on ships at sea for a breather, never a fuckin' cat.'

'Must 'ave bin on board since Le Havre.'

'It's a Frog cat then,' said Mahoney, and Rogers exclaimed with a grin.

'I *like* it, Phoney! I *like* it! We'll call it Froggy.'

'Well,' said Mahoney, after placing an exploratory hand on where he assumed the cat's heart to be. 'I reckon y' can sling it over the wall... it's dead.'

'Dead cats don't mew and I 'eard it mew.'

'Well it ain't gonna mew no more.'

'We'll see 'bout that, smart arse,' said Rogers, transferring the animal to the hotpress which didn't work. 'Cats ain't easily bumped off. It's amazin' it's survived *this* long. If there's a spark o' life…' He returned to his chair and tea as the rest of the 4-8 watch appeared. Suitcase Larson, Nervous Purvis and the Treacle Bender.

Nervous Purvis rolled a cigarette and, bending forward, felt inside the hotpress for the teapot.

'Yahhhhhheeeee!' Leaping back he clung to Rodgers who contemptuously knocked him away. *'There's a rat in the 'otpress!'* he squealed. *'There's a rat in the 'otpress!'* He stared disbelievingly at those present. They were unmoved – even those who had just arrived. Rats at sea were common enough.

'What the fuck's wrong with ya?' he cried. *'Didn't y'ear 'ear wot I said? There's a…!'*

'Cat in the 'otpress,' Rodgers finished.

'Y' mean… *y' know*…? Huhhhh…? A *cat?*'

'An' it's in no condition t'harm yer,' added Mahoney, with a sneer. 'It's fucked.'

'Y' sure?'

'It ain't fucked,' protested Rodgers, and the Treacle Bender began mixing condensed milk with warm water from the heater, which sometimes worked. Emptying salt from a cellar by tossing it over his shoulder, he replaced it with the mixture.

'Wot y' doin'?' asked Purvis suspiciously.

'Wot does it fuckin' *look* like…? Ar'm gonna feed the bastard 'fore it starves… that's wot. Don't suppose the thought entered any of *your* friggin' heads.'

Drop after careful drop was administered until, amazingly, the cat began to feebly lap at the welcome, precious fluid. A cardboard box was then procured for the animal to lie in. Finishing his tea, the Treacle Bender tucked the box under his arm and made for the engine room where he planned to find a cosy spot for the cat in the heat of the stokehold.

'You comin', Phoney?' he called back, as Suitcase Larson and Nervous Purvis made for the wheelhouse and fo'c'sle head respectively.

* * *

The *Susan* had left port without the dubious assistance of the Old Man. The chippie had been called upon by Hercules Duff to somehow gain entrance to his quarters, which were locked. Had the first officer been certain that the Old Man was *in* his quarters and not wandering drunkenly through the streets of Le Havre, he might well have left it at that, but he had to be sure. Expecting to find him in a drink-induced paralysis, he was pleasantly surprised to find him in *shock*-induced paralysis. He was seated cross-legged on his carpet, before an open cognac case, containing a dismantled sub-machine gun and several belts of ammunition.

* * *

The idea had been of epic proportion and had occurred to Mr Duff one morning after Biscay. He had been scanning the distant Portuguese coast from the wing of the bridge when he spun around, face aglow with inspiration, and strode back into the wheelhouse.

'Purvis!' he called. 'Bring her about to starboard!'

'About, chief?'

'Yes man. Hurry. Point her nose in her own wake and keep her there until I instruct you further.'

'Aye, aye, chief.' He began spinning the helm hard over, his brow knit in wonderment. Were they going home again?

Biscay behind them, the Old Man felt well enough to resume his morning visits to the bridge. The gun was assembled and mounted in his dayroom in preparation for any assault upon his private parts by Angus McKenzie. So dispirited by this improvement was Hercules Duff, that he began formulating a plan to re-introduce sobriety in the Old Man by means of more shock treatment. This Christian act deserved his fullest attention and besides, he had been obliged to assume command and it had rested comfortably upon his shoulders.

Simplicity it was. The Old Man would suffer another extended period of incapacity when, on his morning visit top-side, he found the outline of the Portuguese coast to starb'd instead of to port – the ship, in fact, going the wrong way. Instead, what he found was the vessel steaming around in circles as the steering gear, unused to such violent treatment, had gone all to hell. Hours were lost as the chief and second engineer struggled to bring life to the ailing machinery and Chewsday spent hours struggling to bring life to the ailing chief officer.

Hercules Duff had experienced a comparatively privileged upbringing of which he was sometimes ashamed. He was aware that not all children had enjoyed his good fortune. His father had been a successful lawyer, who was also an avid member of every influential club and association in the Hull area where they lived.

From early childhood, the boy had tried to integrate himself as "one of the lads!" The lads, however, wanted little to do with him and were having none of it. They couldn't put a finger on it, but there was something about his pernickety choirboy which did not quite gel with them.

His father had been the very willing recipient of an exceedingly large bonus for proving in a court of law the "Innocence" of a certain shady, wheeler-dealer financier of a charge of corruption. All his experience and expertise had been thrown into the case, as the accused was a member of the same lodge as he, but it transpired that the trial judge, who retired to a villa in the South of France, after the proceedings, was of the same ilk.

This bonus, together with his father's success, enabled the young Duff to attend public school, a minor one, true, none of your Eton and Harrow, more along the lines of your "Goodbye

Mr Chips" variety. British public schools are not in the least bit public, but are pre-eminently private, as private as private schools go, which of course, they are. The children of the proles are sent to the state schools, which are pre-eminently public, as public as public schools go, which of course they are.

To the young Hercules, this sounded as if it had been plucked straight from the pages of "Alice in Wonderland", so he tried not to dwell on it too much, but prayed for godly guidance on the matter.

As a toddler in his pushchair, his nanny would often push him around the local harbours, where they would observe the vessels tied up there. She would point to them and say, 'See, Master Hercules, ships.'

To which he'd respond with, 'Sips.'

'No Master Hercules,' she would insist. 'Ships.'

'Sips.'

'No, ships.'

'No, sips,' he'd repeat.

This continued until that memorable day when she decided to teach him the correct pronunciation. Once more she tried.

'All the *ships*, Master Hercules,' she said, pointing.

'All da sips,' he answered, also pointing. At this point, she'd had enough.

'No, ships,' she said louder.

Actually they weren't ships at all, but fishing boats, but nonetheless.

Applying the brakes on his pushchair, she sank onto her haunches facing him, broad matronly backside only inches from the ground. 'Shhh,' she whispered conspiratorially, fingers to her lips.

'Shhh,' he replied softly, looking into her proud smiling eyes.

'Shhh,' she repeated.

'Shhh,' he also repeated.

'Now ips,' she instructed. 'You know when you fall or knock something over you say "oops".'

'Yes, nanna.'

'Well, now you say "ips".'

'Ips,' he said. And she smiled patronisingly.

'Well, now we put the two together and say ships.'

When he coolly complied, and said, 'ships', she found herself becoming quite unaccountably distraught and began roundly scolding the hapless boy. This unnecessary reprimand ceased the moment she realised just what he'd said. Not sips but ships, and after cursory apologies, she knew he wouldn't understand. She made a point of proudly informing his parents of her success in teaching him a new word.

Nonetheless, the reprimand he'd received simply for being right was not going to be forgotten.

His parents, however, were rarely available to be informed of anything. Not that they wanted to ignore the boy, but always found themselves far too busy attending functions and dinners on behalf of their pet charity, famine relief. They saw their lives as being dedicated to duty and obligation and would happily eat all night in aid of the starving.

Grandfather Hercules Duff had spent most of his working life at sea, so it came as no surprise that the younger of the name, after regularly seeing all the vessels in the harbour, had made up his mind that he, too, wanted to similarly spend his life, but ever since the unaccountable scolding he'd received at the hands of his nanny, its mark had been left and he never again quite knew when he was right or not, even when he was. He would regularly pray for godly guidance on the matter.

He never did become a Freemason, feeling it incompatible with Christianity, they worshipped the architect of the universe! God was much more than that, but the architect of every universe in the well... universe. Heaven, hell, earth and everything that in them is. Therefore, calling Him merely the architect of the universe did not seem to be giving Him his full job title.

* * *

Whilst off duty, the crew amused themselves with cards, chess, draughts, dominoes and, as they were in plentiful supply, racing cockroaches – each wriggling competitor being marked with paint applied with a chewed matchstick. A tobacco tin became the viewing paddock. Froggy the Moggy was now recuperating on the Treacle Bender's bunk. As soon as he was well enough, he removed himself from the crew's quarters altogether and moved amid-ships, where the galley was. He was rarely seen astern again, thus turning his back on those who'd saved his life.

'Ungrateful little bastard!' Mahoney had remarked, but his cardboard box was now a tunnel for the races.

'Phew!' gasped Drunken Duncan. 'This fuckin' cardboard reeks of cat's piss!'

'All the better,' grinned Mahoney, the bookie. 'It should make the little fuckers want t'get outa there… fast.' Then, getting down to business… 'Right lads – for the first race I pay out only evens. Minimum bet twenty fags. No credit and winner only collects… 'ow many runners 'ave we got?'

'Nine,' answered Black Eye McKay.

'Place your bets boys.'

The unwilling participants were tipped into the fashioned tunnel and the entrance blocked. Eager gamblers eyed the only exit. The first to emerge brought a whoop of joy from Big Deal McNiel, who thought it was silver, but which turned out to be white and unbacked.

'Luck o' the draw, fellas,' a smiling Mahoney remarked, as he scooped up his gains. 'Trap 'em for the next race… note down the finishin' order an' I'll offer two t' one on the last four.'

'Why you phoney yella bastard!' snarled Camembert Robert and everyone thought he was referring to Mahoney until he brought down his heel, squashing the insect which had cost him forty cigarettes.

'Tell you wot!' chortled Mahoney. 'I'll offer a thousand t' one on yella for the next race,' and McKay, just then returning from his cabin with more stake, took him on.

Christmas arrived in the Med and the Old Man discouraged any observance by growling 'Bah! Humbug!' to a deputation from the crew requesting a beer issue. The silent night had become a glorious golden morn. Sunshine fell from a cloudless sky to dance in carefree effervescent abandon o'er the rippling aquamarine. A soothing zephyr wafted over the bridge and into the wheelhouse. A morn salubrious, to lie beneath the heavens and luxuriate in their warmth and goodness. A morn to gift the heaviest heart, enthusiasm and ready acceptance of life hereafter.

Hercules Duff, chief mate of the *Susan Snide* and, although he didn't know it yet, of a very wealthy clergyman's widow, had hungrily savoured the sight of the dawning of the most celebrated of all anniversaries. Gaping from the wing of the bridge at sunrise at the spectacle around him, he thought – if this was Earth then how absolutely stupendous heaven must be. This moment was his alone and his heart surged joyously, enraptured with the breathtaking, earthbound glory of it all.

II

In London, the be-whiskered wind of change had blown, devastatingly for some, through the traditionalist heart of the maritime empire, Leadenhall Street. Its direction seemed uncertain, transversing the narrow road of titled wealth and bygone elegance, briefly fluttering the many emblems flying at half-mast in celebration of the passing of one of its noble occupants, and the resultant (expectant), decrease in competition.

Sir Reginald Whippit-Snide, Bart, had gone to that boardroom in the sky. The funeral was barely over when the bunting came down and the takeover bids commenced, based on the assumption that the natural heir, whose outlandish behaviour was well known, would be totally unsuited to the weighty responsibilities of his inheritance, and besides, there was the admirable aspect of saving the famous thoroughfare from possible controversy which may adversely affect business.

Gradually the wind settled on its course, making directly for the Whippit-Snide building, finally petering out in the well-attended boardroom, smog-bound from nervously puffed cigars.

'Henceforth…' Sir Vyvyn K decreed, having expressed his hopes and aspirations for the company and leaving the baying wolves, ravenous for his departure, licking their wounds, '…future assemblies here will take place in the nude. Those not in favour say 'I resign!'

He was well aware that his late father had acquired a considerable reputation as a horny old toad, with young females at head office and far beyond. He was merely redressing the balance. After cruel years of slumber, parliament had awoken and he was free to strike a blow for horny homosexuals. Nor was he even breaking new ground – the Greek and Roman empires were lasting testament to that.

Board meetings were called with increasing regularity, held in camera, for the 'consenting adults' act was still in its infancy. Sir Vyvyn was painfully aware that it would be many years yet before impoverished adult minds emerged from ingrained ignorance. Still, it was not long before news slithered from the inner sanctum, along channels concealed from too wide a hearing, and mysterious men of riches were soon seeking honorary directorships as the clandestine tidings spread. A growing syndicate of tycoons thought naught of flying thousands of miles to attend a meeting or two, in return for entrusting an increasing proportion of the world's cargo to Whippit-Snide holds. The wily new chairman had hit on a winner. Sir Reg would have been greatly impressed.

* * *

The White Horse Tavern in New York's Greenwich Village had witnessed the first meeting of Lady Whippit-Snide and her husband. In those days she'd been the All American product of an All-English mother and an All Scottish father who was a big noise in armaments and getting noisier. With inherent foresight, during the early thirties he moved his business base to England where he delved into politics and soon became involved in trans-Atlantic arms negotiations. Promotion and honours quickly followed.

By 1938 it became evident that his teenaged daughter had inherited his shrewdness. Realising the implications of Teutonic military ambitions, she had decided, whether he approved or not, that England was going to be too dangerous to stay in and was getting the hell out, to the safety of the U.S.A.

She was undoubtedly stunning, and her reflection in the mirror behind the bar leapt to the visiting divorcee's notice. She turned her sweet angelic features towards him after being offered a drink.

'Wotcha want, stoopid?' she enquired. 'If it's wot I tink... I'll tell y' now... I ain't dat kind of a goil... see? Now beat it.'

He was not in the least put out by her response. His heart was indeed beating it, with increasing speed. This was just how he liked them, with lots of spunk. They took a table and he bought drink after drink and she eventually began to loosen up.

'So you're a chip owner, huh?' she asked. He nodded. 'Dat figures... I taught there was somethin' fishy 'bout you.' Her face lit up with sudden inspiration. 'Chip...? Fish...? Geddit?' He joined in her peals of laughter without really knowing why.

'Wotcha doin' in Noo York, anyway?' she asked.

'Oh... business, y'know... takes me all over the place.'

'You married?'

'Er... divorced. And you...?'

'Nope.'

By this time he was mentally undressing her. Superimposing her naked image on that of his luxurious hotel bed. With aching loins and twitching fingertips, he asked, as straightforward as he could. 'Would you... er... like to go somewhere less... er... crowded?' He had been unprepared for such instant success and his blood pressure began to flow increasingly groinwards.

'Okay,' she said nonchalantly, standing up, 'if dat's wot yer want.'

He attempted to gently steer her in the direction of his hotel but she determinedly steered him into another bar which was less crowded.

'Is dat true? You really an English chip owner?' she asked again and he smiled through his disappointment at her doubts.

'Yes... yes, of course.' She sipped thoughtfully, then asked.

'Are you a titled guy, or somethin'?' and his smile froze.

He wasn't a titled guy, or somethin' but he felt he ought to be. The connections were missing. For years now he'd been working on it and out of the blue was his chance about to manifest.

His long, recurring nightmare was that fate had decreed otherwise. An illustrious ancestor had originally instituted the 'Act of God' clause, enabling employers and insurance companies to legally dismiss legitimate claims, thereby saving king's ransoms in pay-outs to the bereaved and industrially crippled. If this hadn't got his forebears into the upper bracket, he'd assumed that nothing would.

'Y'know,' she went on, 'my old man is going to be titled pretty soon.'

'Your old man?'

'Sure, my pop,'

'Your father?' With a look of mild reproof, he chuckled at her innocence. 'Come, come now, my dear. This is the United States. Americans don't...'

'Who said anythin' about my old man bein' a Yank. He's as British as da rest o' you Limeys.'

'What?' This was a startling revelation. 'Your father is British?'

'Yep.'

'Well, I'll be...' He scratched his chin thoughtfully. What a turn of events?

'He woiks in Westminster.'

'In Westminster?'

'Sure... For the government.'

'For the *government*?' His jaw was sagging.

'Yep.'

He was staring at her with growing astonishment. 'Your father is actually employed by His Majesty's Government?'

'Sure,' she shrugged, 'he's... Minister... of Woiks... or somethin'.'

This was incredible. He could see the likeness now. He spoke carefully, fishing his King Edward cigar from the glass into which it had popped with a smoky fizz.

'You mean... he's a British Cabinet Minister?'

'Yeah.'

She picked up her drink as he fell into silent reverie. This beguiling entertainment had now become seriously thought-provoking.

Later, under the influence of alcohol, she recounted her life to date and he quickly concluded that this had been no chance meeting, but pre-ordained. Being a trifle disenchanted with her empty lifestyle, and more than a trifle drunk, she readily accepted his proposal on the grounds that a few German bombs might turn out to be quite exciting, after all.

She even signed up as ambulance crew around London's increasingly battered streets and, over the years, actually grew to love the big stiff.

* * *

Beatrice Pouch had decided that she would like to enter the psychiatric nursing profession, believing such would assist her in the better understanding of her fellow creatures. But more especially those incomprehensible folk at the local DHSS who had caused her much agitation over the years. She found it quite humiliating having her Invalidity Benefit mysteriously periodically cancelled for no apparent reason. She found it all very consternating to the point where mere mention of *them* provoked her more repellent nature. On occasions, callers not instantly recognized had been assumed to be *them* and dealt with accordingly.

While her application was being processed, she was invited to join an informal tour of the wards with other hopefuls at Tooting Bec Hospital. (She had wisely thought it prudent to go in disguise. She possessed several – male and female.)

'Right then,' announced the personnel officer, 'if you will kindly follow me, ladies and gentlemen…'

On Acute Admission, they met Mozart, Sir Henry Irvine and the Pope who blessed them on their departure for the next ward.

'But no Napoleon,' lamented Beatrice to the personnel officer.

'Ah,' he countered with a knowing smile, 'we'll probably find him in Occupational Therapy later,' – which to no one's surprise, they did.

Next on call was the Medium Stay ward where everyone, including the staff, seemed to be smokers and none had any cigarettes. Beatrice, a non-smoker herself, had to face a torrent of abuse from those assuming she was just too tight-fisted to give them any.

Then came the Long Stay ward where they met an old German prisoner of war called Rommel, afraid to go home. The patients were predictably impassive. Blank faces registered the decades of sedated boredom and indifference and the embarrassed visitors responded with silly, self-conscious grins and useless platitudes.

Once on the Psycho-Geriatric ward, their grins were wiped cleanly from faces which viewed the sight with mixed emotions – none of them humorous. Almost all female, (most men being gratefully dead before the onset of 'vegetalia'), they sat around in ill-fitting clothing. Heads lolled or nodded constantly like Jews at prayer, faces locked in muscular spasm, limbs twitched and jerked, urinating and defecating where they sat. Saliva dripped into soaking laps, eyes searching unseeingly beyond time and space. Lips uttered gibberish as doomed minds, once methodically serviceable, responded to visions – things they see and hear which others don't – while overworked and invariably short-handed nursing staff toiled endlessly, bathing, changing and returning their lost charges to their endless dribbling incontinence.

'You will note,' said the personnel officer, sniffing appreciatively as his shocked party held their breath as long as they could, 'that many of these unfortunates are now unable to do anything for themselves.' They collectively agreed with grim, nodding acquiescence.

'Normal communication has broken down,' he went on, 'and there is a very high level of dependency.'

It has to be noted that some of his listeners tried hard to come to terms with the appalling situation. These were, after all, *human beings*, demanding sympathy and understanding. Surely they must have known that people existed who were thus bereft. Yes... they *must* have. They merely hadn't expected to be confronted with them.

Being led into the dining area, they watched as the nursing staff endeavoured to get sustenance into the patients, via spoon and feeder mug.

'During your duties,' the personnel officer continued,' you may see someone who is restless... looks strained... has wet legs. You may notice urine... a pungent smell... Some may even have faeces on their hands which they have wiped onto clothing... even faces... and hair,' he paused. 'Even into their mouths... and it is your task to make these patients comfortable again. Some of this matter may end up on you, as dementia sufferers often cling to the nearest person...'

In the uneasy silence that followed, he saw sympathy in some eyes, and loathing and disgust in others. One young lady promptly vomited where she stood, but, with the aptitude of a trained nurse, blamed it on the nearest patient who was whisked away for an enema.

'If you can't do this,' the personnel officer concluded, 'you will never be a nurse.'

Gratefully they followed him out into the fresher air.

'Well?' he asked, breaking the thoughtful silence that surrounded him. 'What do you think?'

'Only a saint could do this job,' Beatrice declared.

'But they're *all* saints,' he replied proudly, 'in my eyes anyway'.

'I think I should like to become a saint,' said Beatrice eagerly. 'You get to have churches named after you... that sort of thing.'

'Well... er...' He looked at her, eyes half closing in pained perplexity. Was this smart-arsed bitch taking the piss?

'I was speaking metaphorically.'

'Don't you have any *real* saints... y'know... canonization jobs?'

By now the personnel officer had reluctantly concluded that Beatrice was neither a smart arse, nor was she taking the piss. He began to look distinctly uncomfortable and glanced around.

'Surely... I mean...' he hesitantly began, 'for that one must have... er... *visions*... er... see and hear things that others don't.'

'But I *do!*' she exclaimed, with superior delight. He merely gave a knowing smile and winked slyly at the rest of the group.

'Then I've no doubt we'll be seeing you before much longer.'

'You mean...' she gasped happily,'...I've got the job?'

* * *

These were hectic times for the new chairman. Responsibility for his flourishing enterprise entailed strenuous effort and commitment but he was taking steps to lighten the load by delegating more to his growing entourage. All the gorgeous young female staff Sir Reg delighted in, had been replaced with gorgeous young males whom he delighted in.

He had acquired, for the company, a private Caribbean island where he intended, once the New Year had turned, to spend the remainder of the winter and many, if not all, of the winters to come. He had been pleasurably engaged in the selection of companions for the trip, when they came a barely perceptible knock on the door which he had instructed was only to be knocked in a barely perceptible manner.

'Enter,' he called, and in came the head male clerk with the female head.

'Forgive the intrusion sir,' he said, 'but there is an unknown lady downstairs wishing to see you.'

'Oh?' came the reply, eyebrows lifting in surprise.

'She is quite insistent… refuses to leave.'

'If she has an American accent, she's almost certainly my stepmother… Please show her up.'

'I think it's someone else entirely, sir. She speaks West Country and wears a bejewelled cross around her neck.'

'Does she?' he said, looking at him directly. 'Oh, *do* drop this *sir* nonsense. This company is going to leave the rest standing and we are all going to share its success. Now, about this lady…'

'Yes. She wishes to learn when the *Susan* is due in Mombasa and she wants it from the top… you.'

Unknown to his late father, Sir Vyvyn K thoroughly despised the aristocracy and couldn't renounce his title fast enough. A deep and lasting wound had been inflicted by a little known historical fact. Queen Victoria had huffily refused to sign the document outlawing female homosexuality on grounds that such could not possibly exist and with the same quill had rendered the male variety subject to yet a further century of derision, hatred, pilloried persecution and prison. *And they wanted equality*. He could never forgive Oscar Wilde's suffering. They were contemptible. The upper classes were, and still are, hereditarily brain dead.

Full Ahead

'LET GO PORT ANCHOR!' boomed the megaphoned Old Man from the wing of the bridge, and the chippie released the windlass, sending the 'hook' crashing its rusted weight into the calmness of the sea off Port Said. The chain, scraping and rattling its descent, resounded throughout the entire vessel. Here the *Susan Snide* would ride at anchor with a host of other merchantmen awaiting the 0600 hrs convoy through the Suez Canal.

Far into the night, the Old Man impatiently paced the boat-deck. More than whisky would be required to induce sleep when, just across the water, where the lights twinkled annoyingly, there lay, in some agent's office, the bag containing the ship's mail. This could be no ordinary delivery he knew, for amongst letters for his men, there could be something of a very private and confidential nature for himself.

How then could he possibly relax? His tortured mind echoed with self-doubt and mocking recriminations for his unsuitability, his sexual ignorance and failure as a possible suitor; even proposing he abandon the entire venture while some semblance of dignity remained.

* * *

'The Yanks,' said the Snot Gobbler, holding court in the mess, 'if they are to be believed, are bred from bitches, suck each other's cocks on a regular basis and fuck their mothers on the side.'

'I believe 'em,' chimed in Mahoney. 'I was in Greenwich Village a couple o' years back, and this black fella come up t' me – 'is name's immaterial – and said, "America is the richest country in the world, if not the universe".'

''ad y' met this Mr Immaterial before?' asked Black Eye McKay, grinning, and got the snapped response.

'Stop fuckin' me about. I'm serious, anyway he sez "the wealth of this nation is so abundant it's" er...' Mahoney groped for the word, '"incalculable..."' He shrugged. 'I mean... wot was I supposed t' *say*? I was beginnin' t' think it was all some kinda joke but he went on, saying, "The money is pouring non-stop into the States from every corner of the world. The place is awash with the fuckin' stuff." I said 'e was probably right an' y'know wot 'e said t' me...? 'e asked me for a dime for a cuppa coffee. Ah was so impressed wit' 'is patter, I gave the bastard a dollar.'

'Yeah,' sighed The Gobbler, 'but it's all this flag worship that freaks me out. They gottem indoors, outdoors, on their bloody clothes... their cars... y'know...' He added thoughtfully, 'if flags were edible they could all live off the fuckers for a year... maybe more. They've gottem everywhere but on flagpoles up arse'oles... an' that might not be long acomin'.'

'It's all down to brainwashin',' McKay informed them. 'The flag 'as bin rammed down their throats since birth... Jesus is optional, an' would come a poor second in a vote.'

'Look, don' go getting' me wrong or anythin'. I like the Yanks very much. They provide us all wi' so much laughter.'

'Er, wot d'ya mean?'

'Well, take the names some of 'em come wi'. I mean where else would y'find a Hirham J Cocksucker? Begettin' a Hirham J Cocksucker II. Who in turn begets Hirham J Cocksucker III as' so on.'

'Yeah!' McKay drawled tiredly. 'But I hate wot they're doing to the word "Guy". Its bein' strangled t'the point of fuckin' boredom. Everyone's becomin' a fuckin' "Guy" these days over there. Men, women, children, dogs, cats, all the way down to the fuckin' pet tortoise! An' o'course, all their fuckin' brown-nosed followers aroun' the world are followin' suit, including back 'ome.'

'Know what?' The Gobbler enquired.

'Wot?'

'I sailed wi' this Jewish fella on the *Rustenburg Castle* a while back. What a funny fucker 'e was. A laugh a minute. Know wot 'e called 'imself?'

'Now 'ow the fuck would I?'

'The Brick Lane Four Wheeled Skid. 'E came from…'

'Don' tell me, let me guess… er… Brick Lane?'

'Yeah, Aldgate Way.'

'I know where fuckin' Brick Lane is.'

'Anyway, know wot 'e's doin' now?'

''Ow the fuck…?'

''E's a big shot in the Yankie fast food market. Got relatives over there.'

'They usually do.'

'Still a funnier bloke you'd never come across.'

'Yeah,' drawled Mckay again, this time more thoughtfully. 'In the fast food business, is 'e?'

'Yeah.'

'Suppose that's why there's no ham in fuckin' hamburgers. Oh yeah, 'e's funny right enough, but the jokes on us.'

'Still,' said Mahoney, tiring of the topic, 'as long as they're happy.'

But The Gobbler was having none of it.

'If they're all so happy, why d' they keep so many guns?'

'For protection.'

'Against who?'

'Each other, you silly bastard,' said a grinning Mahoney, but The Gobbler wanted the last word.

'Even being right don't make you less a phoney fucker,' he said 'you're as phoney as a workin' class Liverpool entertainer… Y'know the type… can't wait t' hit the big time so they can get on Conservative party platforms.'

'Wot…? Wi' Ted Heath…? You gotta be jokin', or any other Tory for that matter. I'm stayin' Labour.'

'Not wi' Harold Wilson, you're not, 'e's finished. If 'e'd gotten us all involved in this useless Vietnamese slaughter, wi' the bodies mountin' up, they'd be plannin' statues to 'im right now. But 'e refused to, an' saved the lives of countless military personnel, for which the silly bastards probably hate 'is guts. Now you wait an' see... 'e'll be quickly wiped from the plate.'

'Anyway,' broke in the Treacle Bender, feeling ignored, 'I get on okay wi' Yanks... the fellas, I mean. The women piss me off. It's as if they wanna grow balls. They dress like men, walk an' talk like men, refer t' each other as guys an' gun-totting lady police officers couldn't be told apart from men if it wasn't for their tits... an' oh... do those struttin' uniformed harpies just love it.'

'Yeah,' agreed The Gobbler, 'it's as if bein' female is a friggin' violation of their human rights. But they better not forget one thing. It's the screwdriver wot does the screwin'... never the other way 'round. Even when they're on top thinkin' they're fuckin' 'im , the silly bastards ain't. They're just using 'is dick to fuck themselves.'

''eard the latest from the women's movement?' Broke in McKay. 'these short cropped, fat-arsed, jean-clad screaming, men-hating dykes, are now wanting a ban on beauty contests... degrading to women, they sez.

'Yeah...'cos they don't want us seein' 'em, that's why. They want 'em for their eyes only while they finger their manly clits.'

'I read a book once,' McKay informed them. 'about them transsexuals, it was. A woman got changed into a man.'

'Er...' Enquired a curious Gobbler. 'wot d'they call that then?'

''From Knickers to Knackers' or 'Don't be a Cunt all y'life'' He finished without cracking a smile.

'I was in Bay City, Michigan,' remarked the Treacle Bender, 'an' there were notices in the front windows of houses... like... THIS IS AN AIRFORCE HOUSE. HUSBAND A PILOT, an' THIS IS A NAVY HOUSE, SON A MARINE. Can y' just fuckin' imagine this kinda shit in the U.K? THIS IS AN ARMY HOUSE. TWO SONS IN THE PIONEER CORPS.'

'Yeah,' the gobbler went on, 'and what about all the fast food they shovel into their fucking faces, no wonder their public shithouses are called Restrooms.'

* * *

The mail came aboard early with the canal pilot and had been quickly sorted through by Stanley Stone, who, with heavy heart, had concluded that there was none for him. Surely he had, by now, been chief steward of the *Susan* long enough to warrant his promotion to the catering superintendent's office. He approached each port with renewed hope.

'Oh,' remarked Chewsday with surprise, sorting out those for the crew's mess, 'there's one here for the Old Man.'

'What was that?' asked Stanley Stone, instantly alert.

'There's one here for the Old Man... Not company mail. Hand written. It's marked 'Private and Confidential'. He put the envelope to his nose. 'Mmmmm, lovely.'

'Give it here. That's not official ma...'

'No. It's Private and Con...' It was snatched from his hand as Stanley Stone's curiosity overcame him. The Old Man had never before, to his knowledge, received private hand-written mail. And... *perfumed*? Oh... this was too much.

'Shall I take it up to him, chief?' offered Chewsday, helpfully. The reply was instant.

'No, no. I'll see to it. I'll see to it.'

As the convoy slid past Port Said, traders came out, their small bumboats laden with trinkets to be brought aboard, there to make the passage before being lowered over the side again in order to join the north bound convoy.

'Hey then... Johnny!' The Arab was addressing McCall who had been awakened in his bunk by another exited Arab trying to climb in beside him.

'Wot y' want?' he snapped angrily, and was shown the vendor's merchandise displayed upon a hatch cover. The seller grabbed him by the arm but he yanked free.

'You want nice present for girl back home?'

'No.'

'I got plenty stuff, plenty stuff.' Giving his display a dismissive hand-wave, he went on. 'I got more... You come with me.'

Again he took McCall's arm and tried to lead him towards the crew's quarters and again he broke free.

'Oh no y' don't,' he snarled. 'Keep clear o' the accommodation, 'cos if y' don't I'm warnin' ya...'

'But...' hissed the Arab urgently, 'I can't show you here.' He furtively patted the folds of his garment, eyes darting about with well-rehearsed anxiety. 'I got...'

'I *know* wot y' got,' insisted McCall. 'Dirty books an' dirty pictures, you dirty bastard. I've seen and read 'em all, from Mrs Spanker's Academy to...'

'But Johnny...'

'Piss off!'

A bearded Arab was working on Big Deal McNiel. 'Look, Geordie, look!'

His eyes shone expectantly as he held aloft a box of flimsy panties containing a pair for each day of the week. 'For you Scouse, I give very good price.'

'An' who would I give 'em to?'

'To girl.'

'I don't know any girl I could give knickers to.' He paused reflectively. 'Well... maybe just one.' The robed vendor brightened. 'But all seven together wouldn't cover 'er big fat arse.'

'But listen, Yorky...'

'You're givin' me a pain in the...'

'Bollocks!' chuckled Mad McPhee, waving away both seller and merchandise as he made his way back from his stint at the wheel, towards the 'aft accommodation. 'Ar've seen it all before.'

A Highland Scot, he dryly thought it somewhat presumptuous of Lowland Scots wearing kilts and eating haggis on Burns night, when the poet, another Lowland Scot, had probably never done either in his life, as these were highland traditions, troons being the favoured garment among lowland men. But he was also contemptuous of all nationalism, convinced that the flag wavers and anthem singers had unwittingly placed their balls well within the sweaty self-serving grasp of politicians, who then set about transforming themselves from people's representatives to people's rulers. To him anthems and country glorifying songs where simply patriotic insanity with music accompaniment. He thought Mt. Rushmore was the most nauseating edifice in the USA and there were quite a few to pick from. Passing a bumboat cobbler, last between knees, his ears pricked up in an instant – seated upon his collapsible stool he was proclaiming 'Shoes cobbled for free! Shoes cobbled for free!'

This was an opportunity not to be missed and he quickly returned from his cabin with a pair in desperate need of attention.

'Er… you did say these were bein' done for free?'

'Of course, Paddy… Free quid.'

Elsewhere on deck, Mahoney was viewing photographs of indulgent ladies who love ladies.

'You like, Scouse?' enquired the vendor hopefully. Mahoney nodded vaguely. 'You English boy, Taffy?' he went on, receiving another disinterested nod. Spitting on the deck, the Arab declared, 'Americans, shit!'

There was no response so he tried again. 'I take any kinda money – Dutch money, German money, Italian money, French money, Spanish money… any kinda money.'

'Israeli money?' said Mahoney, handing back the photos and wandering off to stunned silence. He turned back. 'Y'know, I can't understan' why you lot and the Jews don't get on better. Y' got so much in common. Middle East origins, good at business… got all the patter… keepin' women in the background where they belong… you won't eat pork, are great showmen and a circumcised prick could open career opportunities in Hollywood.

Mahoney had been on the brink of emigrating to Australia but had abandoned the idea upon realizing that the place was becoming a U.S.A. Mark II (he thought one was enough), complete with men playing that silly girls' game of baseball, where even the fielders wear great leather protective gloves to prevent the little darlings from breaking a fingernail. Any day now he half expected to hear of hairy, sweaty Aussie ockers sentimentally hugging each other in the street, tears of mawkish sentiment in their eyes. Why, even the distinct Aussie hat was being usurped by the Stetson or the equally naff baseball cap. Ah well, he thought, that's show biz. They'll be having the 'Australian Dream' next.

'I tell you wot I do…' a persevering salesman was saying, as Suitcase Larson threw up hands in despair.

'But I've got no bleeding *money*! 'Ow many more times do I 'ave t'…?'

'No matter! No matter! Changey for changey! You got shirt? Jeans?'

'Yeah… an' I'm fuckin' keeping 'em. Now do me a favour an' please…'

'*Piss Off!*' shouted the Snot Gobbler at he who would not take no for an answer.

He had been rudely interrupted, leaning on a rail, quietly flicking flies from the end of his nose with his tongue, deep in private reverie as he watched the desert slip by.

'Listen Tommy,' the Arab whispered into The Gobbler's reluctant ear, 'if you 'shore in Port Said… you look for me, your friend, Abdul. I take you good place… plenty drink… plenty young girls… plenty young boys… any age… Not too much money… Not too much money.'

The Gobbler, like his shipmates, had done the Suez Canal passage many times before and was well conversant with the inventive bumboat patter. He gave a despairing groan.

'Jesus!'

'Christ!' came the cry from Hard Nut Neilson as Chewsday aloofly minced across the deck, obviously in his element. All attempts at peddling ceased immediately as the eyes of Allah's swarthy sons burned with lust at his every lithesome movement, perfected and performed for their delectation and, of course, his own.

Chewsday was good at his job and a likable fellow – kind, helpful, gentle, vulnerable – who had found it paid not to socialize too much with those he didn't know. There were some strange, dangerous people out there of which he wasn't one. At sea he felt as safe and accepted as he would had he been in show business. His shipmates, although invariably his moral and intellectual inferiors, treated him almost as an equal. He was grateful for that and his rehearsed mince across the deck had been done merely to provide some entertaining light relief. Involved in a long-term relationship back home, where they were buying their own flat, previous promiscuity was not the driving force it had, unashamedly, once been. But occasionally, his need to express himself in a noticeably colourful manner got the better of him.

The international convoy moved slowly on through a landscape of sand, relieved only by the occasional labourers working in groups alongside the canal, their ever patient camels squatting nearby, or the sight of a dredger endlessly dragging up silt in the process of deepening and widening the invaluable channel.

The pilot had tried, unsuccessfully, to engage the Old Man in conversation as he moodily paced the bridge, his anxiety even worse than on the previous evening. He had expected *some* hindrance, that was the story of his life, but not in the shape of a competitor for Beatrice's undoubted charms – some bloody upstart called Sam who had the advantage of living in the same blasted building as she.

* * *

The Red Sea voyage was hot and breezeless. Moreover, although few were surprised to see them, the rats started appearing. Nineteen seventy-three received a miserable welcome, especially from the Scot's contingent who sadly recalled Hogmanays of such duration that no one knew or cared which year it was. With the intensifying heat, the Old

Man had issued a warning that anyone failing to take adequate precautions and suffering sunburn to a degree which would hinder the carrying out of their duties, would be heavily logged.

If it was hot and close topside, down in the engine-room it was much, much worse. As the mercury climbed, handrails and guardrails were becoming too hot to hold onto for long and would soon become painful to touch. Heat from the deckplates seeped through boots in which feet squelched in sweat which trickled in rivulets down weary legs. Sweat rags were tied loosely around necks beneath blinking dripping faces like boiled lobsters. Ahead lay Aden, then the wider but no cooler expanse of the Indian Ocean beckoned as the *Susan Snide* cut cleanly through the flat-calm glassy sea.

Extremely hot too was the galley, with the added discomfort of flies hovering around the cook's head as sweat dripped from his nose into the soup cauldron. Behind him, dark hands and face dusted white with flour, the baker cursed vehemently as he worked.

'Oh, these poxy flies 'ave bin driving me doolally since Port Said.' He shook his head vigorously to thwart an attempted landing, sprinkling the dough with sweat. 'It's as if the frigging bastards are all engaged in systematic torture.'

'Yeah, well...' the cook drawled, '...I mean... wot the fuck d' ya expect? They're *Ayrab* flies... worst in the fucking world is *Ayrab* flies.'

'Y' reckon?'

'Take my word on it.'

''Orrible bloody things.'

'There ain't a filthier thing on earth... Y'know, they can't swallow first time round... They sorta chews, half swalla, then bring the whole fuckin' mess up in vomit, then they can eat it.'

'Christ!'

'So when y' see one on y' dinner an' chase it off, it's too late mate, it's already spewed.'

'Yuk,' shuddered the baker, 'if only they weren't so bleedin' quick.'

'Mmmmmm,' the cook agreed with a knowing nod. 'It must be all the practice they get buzzin' 'round camels' arseholes... dodgin' waggin' tails.'

'Yeah... waitin' for the ultimate pleasure... a fart.'

'Oh no,' said the cook in emphatic disagreement, 'no, surely... when the camel shits... *that's* the ultimate pleasure. I mean... look 'ow much longer it lasts.'

His galley mate could not dispute this and the cook went on.

'Y' know somethin' else...? It's kinda strange... people – especially women, 'ave all sorts of phobias an' I'll bet spiders are top o' the list. Spiders!... clean harmless things wot kill the fuckin' flies! Yet 'ow many silly bastards 'ave phobias about flies?'

'Not many, I suppose.'

'Right,' the cook agreed. 'I asked 'im,' (meaning the chief steward) 'for something to kill the bastards but he sez we can't use it in the galley... poisonous, he sez.'

The baker snorted. 'an wot abart the fuckin' flies... ain't *they* poisonous?' He brought down his hand in a resounding slap, burying an unseen fly in the dough.

The second cook and baker – to give him his correct title – had begun his seafaring life years before as an assistant steward on the *Durban Castle*. His parents had come to Britain from Jamaica, settled in London's East End where he was born and he never tired of recounting his first visit to South Africa. Ignorant of the apartheid system, he'd gone ashore in Capetown with a shipmate from Liverpool, only to learn that they were not allowed to partake of beer in the same bar, there being those for whites and those for non-whites. As many cans as they could carry had been purchased from a liquor store. Then they took the cable car to the summit of Table Mountain where they drank all the beer and emptied their bladders in as many places as possible. They had also heartily vomited up there too and came down feeling much the better for it.

'It's alright for 'im...' he grieved on, 'sat under his fan all day...'

'Or flat on 'is back... pumpin' 'imself,' added the cook.

'What? There isn't a decent wank in the sod.'

'Well, I suppose the bottom line is... as long as 'e keeps outa our bloody way.' The cook stooped to inspect the Lancashire Hotpot, bubbling in the oven. 'The less we see of 'im the better. *Lookin'* like a comic don't make 'im funny.'

'Wot? 'E's got as much humour in 'im as your mate.'

The cook frowned. 'My mate?'

'The Old Man, o' course.'

'The Old Man...? My mate...? Are you crazy?'

'Well, I mean...' the baker drawled, grinning slyly, 'wot are we t' think? Two days adrift in Antwerp an' not even *bollocked*... let alone, logged!' He tossed his dough heavily onto the bench where two flies were busy performing their last reproductive act.

'*You* were adrift as well,' the cook retorted in hurtful tone.

'For three hours... that's all... *and* I made up the time.'

'Well... 'e's no mate o' mine.'

'Then 'ow do y' account for...?'

The cook turned to face him, tapping his nose with a forefinger.

'Never you mind.'

'Wot sort of answer is that?'

'I'll tell y' somethin' else,' chuckled the cook, or rather, sniggered... 'I'll be adrift in Mombasa too.'

''E'll throw the book at ya.'

'No 'e won't.'

'Who says?'

'*I* do.' The cook laughed aloud at the astonished face of the baker.

'*Now* who's crazy?'

'Wanna know why?'

The baker nodded and was told.

''E's afraid I'll stick my dick in 'is dinner.'

Raising and flinging down the dough once more, the baker turned to stare at the cook, open-mouthed.

'An' would ya?'

'Certainly not, you filthy bastard.' The cook straightened with indignation, as far as his hump allowed. 'I'll 'ave you know I take pride in everythin' I ...'

'Cook!' came the cry, making them both start.

Stanley Stone stood in the doorway, immaculate in tropical whites, knobbly knees exposed and two gold braids on each sloping shoulder. His splendour was only slightly marred by an ugly darkening swelling on his forehead.

Burning with curiosity about the mysterious sender of the Old Man's perfumed letter, and shuddering with dread that it might be from a certain powerful person at head office, despite the unmistakable feminine hand (had Sir Vyvyn become *Dame* Vyvyn via the scalpel?) he had been caught feverishly steaming it open in the saloon pantry by the Old Man. The foulest of tempers was upon him for he had received no personal mail in the delivery so, with bottle and glass in hand, he was looking for ice. What met his blazing eyes brought him roaring in, swinging the bottle with angry precision. Then he thundered out while the luckless steward picked himself up, thankful that the Old Man had forgotten the ice for he would need it for his head.

'Er... wot can I do for *you*... chief?' enquired the cook, hastily drowning his cigarette in the soup and accidentally knocking over the saucepan in which boiled his underpants. As the contents spilled onto the hot surface of the stove, the galley filled with caustic steam. Stanley Stone haughtily pinched his nose as the two gasping men stumbled out, pushing past him, to slump over a rail and inhale greedily the unpolluted air.

'When you have finished contaminating the ship with your incompetence,' he called after them, 'I'll tell you that the Old Man does not desire Lancashire Hotpot.'

'And wot, pray,' asked the cook, voice thick with sarcasm as he turned to curtsey lopsidedly, 'is the master's preference?'

'Goulash.'

'Then goulash it shall be, yessiree.'

The chief steward thankfully departed and the smile of insincerity vanished from the face of the cook who returned to dispose of his smouldering underwear and use the overturned pan for the new dish.

''E' shall 'ave 'is fucking goulash,' he snarled.

'With nobs on,' echoed the baker.

'Or *in* it,' agreed the cook.

It wouldn't have mattered anyway. The Old Man didn't want goulash or anything else. But as logging the cook was out of the question, he was giving him extra work to do.

II

'There are no rats aboard my ship!' he yelled at Hercules Duff, who had innocently passed on information received from the deck and engine crew. *'If there are... then they are of the homo sapiens variety!* Sly conniving rats. Scrotum squashing rats, whisky diluting rats and...' he glared through slits of disgust and loathing, '...amoral, depraved, perverted rats who flout the rules of public decency.'

'Oh, but sir...' rejoined the mate, looking uncomfortably at his shoes, 'I certainly wouldn't have placed you in that... er... category.'

Rampant with indignation, the Old Man heard not a word.

'Everyone aboard but me has life *too bloody easy,*' he declared. 'They think this is some kind of *pleasure cruise*! Well, I've got news *for the lot o' you*, Mr Duff. This is the *Susan Snide,* not the blasted *Saucy Sue!'* He paused to pour himself a drink, only to forget what he was talking about.

* * *

He had shut himself away and flopped on his bed, admiring the heavenly aromatic envelope he had wrested from Stanley Stone, his heart racing, eyes aglow with excitement. This was his very first letter from Beatrice, indeed, his first ever from *any* lady. He'd pace, then flop, pace, then flop some more, expecting he knew not what but finding the experience so pleasurable he was tempted to prolong it even further by not opening the envelope.

His chest swelled with self-admiration as he drank in his reflection in the full-length mirror on his wardrobe door. Only when he felt the momentous occasion was upon him, did he reach, trembling, for the letter opener. Once in his hand, the gathering storm of counter accusation rose insidiously to mar his joy and his frown was one of pain-filled irritation.

'Yes, I damned-well *am!*' he exclaimed through clenched teeth at his reflection's silent proclamation. 'I am perfectly well-balanced.' Reassured by his self-assessment, he wobbled towards the bed on which he sat, preparing the grand opening.

'Stop! Stop at once! Do you hear?' He gagged, and the envelope fluttered from his grasp.

'Who...?' He got up, returning to the mirror, peering into it. 'What did you say?'

'You heard me.'

'But why?'

'You are not in a fit condition to read it, assimilate the contents and compose a suitable reply, one which will do you credit.'

'But, hang on, here...'

'Don't you realize the importance of the situation, man? A young lady of, I suspect, great charm and virtue, has taken the time and effort to contact you and you're too arrogant to allot the attention it deserves... She has *written* to you, you old sod. Something not even your mother did. Do you appreciate that?'

'Oh yes,' he sighed tiredly, running a fluttering hand across his worried brow, then made for the bottle. Propped up on a pillow, Tedward looked on as he eased himself into a chair. The glass had barely touched his lips when suddenly his eyes grew round with comprehension and his shoulders squared determinedly. What on earth...? How could...?

Picking the letter up he declared, 'I'm going to *read* the bloody thing, whatever *you* think.' He began to chuckle. Why, the very idea. It was ludicrous. 'Stop me if you can!' he cried. When there was no response he went on triumphantly... 'You CAN'T... CAN YOU?' He slapped his thigh in joy. 'And I know WHY!' he cackled, crying uncontrollable tears of relief. *'You can't bloody stop me because you don't exist! You're just a REFLECTION and I'm over here, out of your line of vision!'* With unmitigated joy he winked victoriously at Tedward, who winked victoriously back. *'I've got you licked, you bastard! You are no more!'*

'Oh, but I am,' replied the mirror, softly, and the Old Man's glass dropped to his feet.

'You CAN'T be!' he wailed. 'I'm no bloody ventriloquist... *am I* Tedward?'

'Outa the question,' agreed Tedward.

'Anyway,' the mirror continued, 'I'm not preventing you from reading it.'

'You're not?'

'Certainly, my dear fellow.'

'You really *mean* that?'

'Indeed, Bix, old boy.'

'Don't be bloody impertinent.'

'Aren't *we* touchy today?' the mirror chided. 'Anyway, as I said, I won't stop you because I have no right.'

'That's right,' the Old Man declared, nodding vigorously, 'you have no right.'

'All the same,' came the thoughtful response, 'you should not jeopardise, or possibly scuttle, your one and only chance of a lasting, worthwhile and ... who knows... possibly *productive* relationship.'

'What do you mean...' replied the Old Man, lurching over to peer into the mirror, '...scuttle?'

'Well... you may write the wrong thing, or even the right thing in a way that conveys a different meaning. You may forget what you wrote, or even *that* you wrote. You need a clear head and full control of your faculties to study this letter and compile a suitable reply.'

'But I'm perfectly capable.'

'I grant that you have kept to your own perspective of moderation.'

'That must prove *something?*'

'It does… you're pissed.'

'*I'm* not taking this from a *mere mirror*,' the Old Man snapped. 'I refuse to hear anymore. You've talked yourself into a watery grave, smart arse.' And he strode out with nary a backward glance.

* * *

The first to meet a rat was Nervous Purvis. He was roused for his watch at 0400 hrs and went to the mess, as usual. Still drowsy, he groped inside the hotpress which didn't work, for the teapot and extracted what his half-asleep brain had assumed to be the cat and found himself staring, horror-struck, into burning rodent eyes.

'*Wot's up? Wot's up?*' cried Mad McPhee, another of the early watchkeepers, arriving, who'd heard his shrieks from the stern.

'A rrrr… *rat!*' wailed Purvis. '*Not a cat… a fuckin' rat… I picked the bastard up! Ohhhhh!*'

'Snap out o' it, you prick!' he yelled, as Mahoney arrived on the scene, armed to the teeth with a Falcon pipe.

'It's *there*, ah tell ya… it ran under the 'otpress… If y' don't believe me, LOOK… GO ON… LOOK!'

'Under the 'otpress?'

'Yeah, an' the fucker's still there… or I'm a Spaniard.'

Warily, McPhee dropped to his knees before the hotpress as a puzzled Mahoney, ignorant of the situation, looked on.

'Be careful,' Purvis instructed, 'it's a big bastard!'

McPhee duly looked with care under the hotpress.

'Can y' *see* it? Can y' *see* it?'

'The only big bastard aroun' 'ere is *you*,' announced McPhee. 'There's fuck all there.'

'But it *was* there! I even 'ad 'old of the friggin' thing!'

The men sat down to his loud persisting. 'It *was*. I tell y' it was THERE! Wot in the name o'Christ d' ya think I am… eh… crazy?'

'You're a Spaniard,' growled McPhee.

Determined to prove himself under the watchful eyes of those present, Purvis strode bravely to the hotpress, grabbing the broom as he went. Steeling himself, he bent far over and thrust the broom handle underneath, sliding it first one way, then the other. He felt nothing. Could the crafty rat be hurdling over the moving broom? Dropping to his knees he quickly scanned the darkened area – apart from the cockroaches… nothing. He felt empty. Climbing sadly to his feet, he gasped.

'Mama Mia! Una cervasa blanca! Cuanto costa senorita?'

But he needn't have worried. His Britishness was re-established later when Froggy proudly flung the dead rat across the mess room deck.

'The 'ot weather brings 'em out,' remarked Downtown Daley knowledgeably, 'looking for water.' Just as they themselves had been brought out to arrange their mattresses on hatch covers in order to sleep under the coolness of the night stars.

'I don't like it,' said Black Eye McKay, lying on his mattress. 'Suppose they get into the galley… I wouldn't put it past the cook t' drop one in the stewpan.'

'Froggy'll sort 'em out, you'll see,' the Treacle Bender assured them confidently.

'They could be company spies,' said Odd Ball McCall, who did not seem to be joking. He went on in hushed tones. 'They've probably got transmitters down there, sendin' nightly messages…'

'Brainless wanker,' scoffed Hard Nut Neilson, sniggering. 'Where the fuck would they get transmitters from?'

'Search me.'

'Whoever 'eard o' rats bein' spies, you gormless…'

'Wot about Hartlepool, then? They hung a monkey as a spy there once.'

'Mmmmmm.' There followed a period of thoughtful silence. They had all heard of this from various Hartlepool shipmates over the years, so it must be true.

'Well…?' McCall said at last, '…if a monkey can do it, so can a rat.'

Then the engine-room storekeeper shot up from the bollard on which he'd been sitting strumming his guitar, ears cocked. The constant throbbing of the vessel's pulse had ceased.

'Breakdown,' he murmured as they slid to an unscheduled stop.

* * *

'Er... excuse me, sir,' ventured Hercules Duff, with considerable courage. He had been waiting for some time and his feet ached. 'Mind if I sit down?'

'Help yourself,' the Old Man replied.

'Er...' the mate continued, gratefully settling himself, 'do you suppose that... Mr McKenzie isn't coming?'

'Not coming?' The Old Man was quite astonished. 'When I send for somebody, somebody comes... that's if they know what's good for somebody... by jingo, yes!'

'But surely sir... I mean... he'll be down in the engine-room, directing repairs.'

'Like bloody hell, he will!' the Old Man winced, after a large gulp of scotch. 'Oh... he'll be down there alright, but as for directing repairs... I wouldn't be surprised if there were none to direct.'

'But sir...'

The Old Man silenced him with a reproving finger and a dismissive shake of the head.

'Listen,' he said, 'I'm going to give you some useful advice for when command comes your way.'

Advice from the Old Man was rare indeed and the mate leaned eagerly forward. His interest vanished, however, when the Old Man added, 'Remote though it is'. He poured another drink and went on. 'Never trust engineers. They stop at nothing to discredit us. Don't get too familiar with them either... breeds contempt y'know. And the chief is invariably the worst of the lot. Take McKenzie for example, I ask you... Not content with being the highest paid officer aboard, next to me, he actually has the gall to think himself...'

'Yes... quite, sir,' the mate sighed tiredly, unable to hide his disappointment. This was nothing more than another salvo in the idiotic, never-ending feud, which, like the battle of the sexes, had little justification. 'But what has this to do with the breakdown sir?'

'Elementary, my dear Duff... Elementary.'

'Sir?'

'Don't you see?'

'I must confess, I don't.'

'I believe there *is* no breakdown.'

'But she's *stopped*,' came the puzzled response.

'And what does *that* prove?' The Old Man watched as across his desk, a chin was scratched in thought.

'Do I read you correctly sir?' he asked at last. 'You suspect him of deliberately impeding the vessel's progress for reasons of his own?'

'And why not? He hates my guts, y'know. I shall log the bastard for it when he gets his arse up here.' He stabbed his finger at the logbook.

'For hating your guts?'

'No, no. I couldn't get away with that, even though I *do* hate his guts. But I'm going to log him each time the engine fails to respond to orders. This vessel will maintain her schedule if it costs him every penny. I will entertain no excuse.'

Again the mate sighed wearily, and coughing politely into a relaxed fist, said 'Well that's quite an allegation sir. In all my years, I've never heard of an engine being stopped at sea unnecessarily.'

'And how the hell do you know?' the Old Man challenged. 'What makes you so sure?'

'Well... I mean...'

'Don't be silly Mr Duff. You don't know at all. You're just surmising. Have you ever checked up?'

'Not... er... exactly, no.'

'Therefore you don't know.'

'But surely,' he persisted, 'it's a matter of trust.'

'Trust? I wouldn't trust McKenzie as far as I could kick him. All we hear either comes over the engine-room phone or from the chief engineer who comes strolling up here as if he couldn't give a shit whether we move or not. He then launches into a load of codswallop about pumps and boilers and so on, which could have been avoided in the first place with a little competence.' He angrily slapped the desktop. 'And all the while we must await *their* bloody pleasure! It's downright *humiliating*, especially for *ME!*'

'Nevertheless sir,' murmured the mate, 'breakdowns do occur and…'

'Many years ago,' said the Old Man, leaning back where he sat, stroking his furrowed brow with trembling fingers, 'I had to go down to an engine-room for some reason, during a breakdown. I don't know what I expected but I was quite unprepared for what I found… which was nothing.'

'Nothing at all, sir?' gasped Hercules Duff. 'But… where had the engine gone?'

The Old Man groaned in despair.

'Not nothing, *nothing*, y'fool. Nothing, *no one*! Not a soul in sight. I finally traced them to the shaft tunnel…'

'Ah!' he nodded 'where the fault was.'

'You're not often right, Mr Duff, but you're wrong again. They were playing bloody cards! The chief, a hideous specimen if ever I saw one, snarled into my ear like Humphrey Bogart at his most menacing.' To illustrate his point, the Old Man rose and grasped the shirtfront of the mate, drawing him some way across the desk, and hissed into his ear. 'One word to anyone and you'll be taken from your bunk one dark night and tossed over the wall.'

The startled mate was bleating for forgiveness and promising not to utter a word when the Old Man pushed him away before pulling him angrily back.

'*I'm only acting!*' he cried, and the quivering mate sank back, sighing thankfully. It was a moment or two before composure was regained.

'And did you report the matter sir?' he asked.

'Did I hell? I'm not suicidal. I was only fourth mate at the time. Those bastards would have had me for sure.'

Mr Duff looked somewhat perplexed.

'Er... forgive me but... why... I mean why the subterfuge? They could have played cards with the engine running.'

'Oh there was motive all right. We were two days from Glasgow where we were to spend a couple of days loading. It was mid-week arrival and they had decided, for sordid reasons no doubt, that it suited their purposes to arrive Friday. Oh, you've got to watch 'em... Bastards everyone! Incapable of intelligent thought as we know it, but devious to a man.'

His glass hovered mid-way to his lips.

'Incidentally,' he said, 'did you get the men over the bow and stern, repainting her name?'

'Yes, sir. They didn't like it.'

'I never thought they would,' he replied with a snigger, 'but the rust had all but obliterated it.' He looked uncertainly at the mate, who looked uncertainly back. 'You're not being a trifle too easy on them, I hope?'

His response came quickly, eager to dispel this notion.

'Oh no, sir. I can assure you of that. Why, only the other day I overheard one of them refer to me as... er... a...' His face suffused in crimson embarrassment. The Old Man was agog.

'Well...? Out with it... What did he say?'

Swallowing hard, Hercules Duff continued softly. 'He called me a... a... F.C., sir.'

The Old Man rose dreamily to his feet and toyed with his empty glass.

'He said that?'

'Oh, indeed, yes. I swear it, sir.'

The Old Man sat again, lounging contentedly, viewing his second in command with something just short of affection. Surely Robert couldn't have been right.

'Er... anything else, Hercules?' he asked with frightening tenderness.

'Well... he... he...'

'Yes... go on.'

'He... he...' He was fidgeting uneasily and casting about for speedy escape routes.

'Come, come now, Hercules,' urged the Old Man with such a reassuring smile the mate's blood became ice. 'We've been together for far too long for the harbouring of silly secrets. Come now, oh trustworthy one... what did he say?'

'Well... he... mentioned that you were a... a... F and a B, sir... and... and... the biggest C at sea, sir.'

'Excellent!' came the joyful cry. 'Excellent!' He slapped the desk, shaking with silent laughter. 'Hercules, my dear, dear fellow, you've quite made my day.'

* * *

The second engineer had heard the scream over the engine noise. Fearing that his donkeyman, whom he'd last seen leaning over the guardrail into the engine space in order to check the temperature of a bearing with his hands, had fallen into the crankpit below, he came running, face as white as his new boiler suit.

'What's the hell's the score?' he yelled, obviously enraged to find Mahoney still alive and well. 'I thought you were down the crankpit.'

'Crankpit?' queried Mahoney, puzzled. 'You did'n tell me t' get down the crankpit.'

'I know I didn't tell y' t' get down the crankpit.'

'Then why are y' saying I should be down the crankpit?'

'I'm *not* sayin' you should be down the crankpit. I just thought...'

Mahoney waved a reproving finger.

'That's wot y' said... I thought you was down the crankpit.'

'Why, for Chrissakes, would I want y' down the crankpit? You crackpot.'

His temper was rising.

'Dunno,' shrugged Mahoney. 'First y' did'n tell me t' get

down the crankpit an' then y' say why ah'm not down there. Ah'll do whatever y' say, second, that's mah job, but first y' gotta tell me. 'Ow was I t' know I was supposed t' be down the crankpit when…?'

'Ah didn't want y' down the fuckin' crankpit!'

'But you sez…'

The engineer threw up his hands.

'Okay, Mahoney, you asked for it. Get down the crankpit.'

'Now?'

'The sooner the better.'

'Well, if that's wot y' want.'

'Too bloody right.'

'Okay… Head first, feet first… or wot?'

'I don't give a shit.'

'Tell y'wot!' he exclaimed, inspired. 'I'll go in sideways. I'll lay on the rail 'ere, 'old onto this bearin', then just… sorta… roll in. 'Ow about that?'

'Just do it.'

'Fair do's.' He put on a pair of asbestos gloves. The onlooker was curious.

'What are those for?'

'So I don' burn maself on this bearin' 'ere. It's running bloody 'ot, y'know. That's why I screamed before. I laid my hand on the bastard.'

Mahoney was about to mount the guardrail as promised when the engineer leapt forward to drag him back. Leaning over the rail himself, he felt the suspect bearing and jumped back, blowing on his scorched hand.

'Water!' he bellowed. *'Get water, quick! Toss it over this bearin' by the bucketful!'*

Wispy smoke was emerging where the stationary bearing met the spinning shaft. Wide-eyed, he rounded on Mahoney again. *'GET MOVIN'… NOW!'*

'Not me. I'm gon' down the crankpit.'

'You'll do as I say.'

'Yeah… Get down the crankpit, you sez.'

'Ah'm ORDERIN' ya!'

Mahoney thought that he had better do as bid and made off in the direction of the seawater cock.

The battle of the bearing lasted throughout the watch – water first being tossed over it, then poured onto layers of cotton waste to soak it, retaining its coolness a little while longer. The Treacle Bender had been summoned from the stokehold to lend a hand which prevented, for a time anyway, further deterioration as the race wore on. An eternity later, eight bells sounded and an unhappy Downtown Daley, with Blackeye McKay, took over. They lost the battle within thirty minutes as the bearing's soft silver lining began to ooze forth and drip from the spinning shaft into the crankpit below. By now Angus McKenzie had been notified. He ordered the engine stopped and all his men below.

Chainblocks were speedily rigged above the disabled bearing to haul it clear of the shaft before it cooled sufficiently to re-solidify, welding bearing to shaft. The air was already thick with sweat and curses when the phone rang, not unexpectedly.

'It's the Old Man, chief,' announced the second, holding a hand over the phone. 'He wants you topside right away.'

'Balls!' snapped Angus McKenzie, not taking his eyes from the job in hand. 'Tell 'im, balls.'

He was incensed. A stinking, blasted, poxy breakdown in the stinking, blasted, poxy Red Sea was all he stinking, blasted, poxy needed. Having to put to sea at all was bad enough. The elation experienced at his elevation to the flagship had lasted only until he learned the new master's identity.

He was sick of ships and engine-rooms, appalled that he still had to mix with dirty, sweaty, foul-mouthed men in dirty, sweaty foul-smelling overalls. In addition were the loathsome fumes and stink of boilers, noisy machinery, grease, grime, oil and filth. And the heat... the abominable heat... the filthy, foul, stinking, blasted poxy heat. Even though he only went below now when it was absolutely unavoidable, he knew it was there and that was bad enough.

Surely the author of his destiny would soon cast him in a

more suitable, deserving role. One of prestige, of paperweights, messengers, telephones without obnoxious deck officers at the other end, pens, inkwells, swivel chairs, filing cabinets and trays marked 'IN' and 'OUT'. There would be typewriters with chattering, clean-mouthed, perfumed, tight-breasted, efficient, bespectacled secretaries knocking hell out of them and making him delicious cups of aromatic coffee in the shore superintendent engineer's office. Sighing dreamily, he took his pipe from a pocket, sucked on it thoughtfully, instinctively testing for blockages. Satisfied, he applied a match and drew deeply, but not in the least, contentedly.

They finally got underway again at 0500 hrs and at 0800 hrs, as many prepared for a well-earned breakfast, the Old Man, still smarting over the delay, rang down 'STOP'. This caused panic below where all assumed that collision was imminent.

'Mr Duff,' the Old Man informed the tired mate, who'd been summoned. 'I've logged Angus McKenzie a week's pay in his absence and shall now inflict my revenge on the rest.'

'Er...'

'Sound the alarm for lifeboat stations. I want a full drill.'

Angus McKenzie, divining blatant one-upmanship, flatly refused to co-operate and was further logged, again in his absence.

Port and starb'd boats were lowered and ordered to make a complete circuit of the drifting vessel. Second mate, Thorndyke Camp, skippered the starb'd boat with the third engineer, as it boasted a motor which was due to be tested, even though the Old Man had ordered only oars to be used. Still, the engineer had received his instructions from the chief and removed his lifejacket to more easily swing the starting handle.

'Ready when you are, Thorndyke,' he called, and received the nod from the second mate seated by the tiller.

With gusto and vigour, he attacked the starting handle – fumes spluttered from the upright exhaust making him gasp as he swung, faster and faster with more and more effort, too intent to notice the handle slipping from the spindle. The stubborn machinery was about to burst into life and did so as he, with a cry of horror, toppled backwards into the drink.

'I can't swim!' he called, breaking the surface only to resubmerge, and the second mate kicked off his shoes and leapt to the rescue.

'Right, you bastards!' yelled the bosun, *'this is it!'* He sprang for the tiller, eyes ablaze with manic excitement. *'Quick! Get this fuckin' tub into gear!'* Mad McPhee grabbed the lever and with a sigh, the craft chugged quietly away.

On ranted the bosun. 'Workin' all day an' most o' the night! Rats takin' over! No beer! No rum! Not even iced water! An' now no fuckin' breakfast! I've 'ad enough! Stuff 'em all! Let's get t' fuck outa here…! *More speed! More speed!'*

McPhee altered the lever and their speed increased.

'That's more like it!' the bosun cackled, eyes shining as he bobbed up and down ecstatically. 'Yes… Yeah y' bastards… *THAT'S* more like it!'

'Er…' began Hard Nut Neilson, after several tranquillizing moments, 'I'm er… not trying t' put a damper on y' day, or anything bosun… but just where the fuck are we goin'?'

'We're getting' t' hell outa here.'

'Yeah… but where?'

'Any bloody where.'

'Where's *that* supposed t' be?' asked One Way Rodgers, who normally didn't say much at all but was obviously unimpressed. He'd once been told that he was so boring he could talk himself to sleep. He'd tried it and it worked. 'This could be a one way trip to nowhere.'

'Well that should suit *you*,' Drunken Duncan declared. 'You've skinned outa more ships… no one expects y' to return to the U.K. on the one y' left.'

'That's not true, anyway…'

'Hey!' cried Duncan, suddenly inspired. 'Let's smash open the emergency supplies. There's bound t' be some booze.'

'I'm no fucking Cap'n Bligh,' the bosun raved on, 'but I'll

get us somewhere… just leave it t' me lads. Just leave it…'

'*MR CAMP! MR CAMP!*' The Old Man's amplified fury bellowed over the placid sea. *'BRING BACK THAT BLASTED BOAT… D'Y HEAR?'*

Almost two miles had been covered before pursuit began. The struggling survivors had been plucked from the briny, the portside lifeboat had been hauled aboard into its davits and the Old Man had smashed a couple of wheelhouse windows. Smoke belched thick and black, rising obscenely into the clear blue sky as Downtown Daley, unaware of the pandemonium, flashed up the furnaces.

So, it's finally come to this, thought a disheartened Oddball McCall at the helm, cursing Neilson's name. After all they'd been through together; all the trips they'd made together. Many good times, some less good, but always shared… the loggings they'd paid and how often had he declined to sign on because there wasn't a berth for Neilson. All the world-wide piss-ups they'd had together – from Joe Beef's bar in Montreal to Ma Gleeson's in Auckland – from the Martinique in Rio Grande de Sol to the Borneo Bar in Sibu, Sarawak… ah yes, memorable all, if only they could remember them. Why… they'd even had a dose of gonorrhoea together… *and* from the same girl too! But for what…? So that he could skin out in the middle of the Red Sea without him?

His doleful reflections were shattered by the Old Man charging through the door. Gesticulating wildly, with clenched fist pointed through the broken glass, he shrieked, *'FOLLOW THAT BOAT!'* before dashing for the telegraph to ring down 'FULL AHEAD'. He then ran out onto the starb'd wing, cursing like a mad man and waving not one, but two angry fists at the sky.

The screw began its turn, slowly at first, causing gentle whirlpools on the glassy water which soon became churning, bubbling, hissing, thrusting activity, totally alien to the glassy surface as far as the eye could see astern, up ahead it was different. The vessel gave a shudder as if awoken from forbidden sleep and slid off as bid.

'Never,' whined Hercules Duff, entering the wheelhouse from the chartroom, where he had deliberately escaped the Old Man's wrath, and wringing hands as head shook in wide-eyed disbelief. 'Never in all my years, have I *known* such a thing.'

'Nor me chief,' McCall agreed sadly.

'Had I not witnessed it with my own eyes…' He then gasped and childishly stuffed fingers into his mouth to stifle a scream. 'Oh my God, NO!' He was looking, with increasing horror, to where the Old Man was now lumbering across the foredeck, drunkenly brandishing his sub-machine gun as he made his way to the fo'c'sl head.

'*He's actually going to…!*' By now McCall had seen him too. The mate spun to face him.

'*We must not allow the ship anywhere near the lifeboat!*' he shouted.

'Sorry chief, the Old Man wants 'em caught.'

'But the *consequences*, man!'

'Sorry chief.'

'But you don't understand,' the mate hissed, he's *armed.*'

'With arms?'

'Yes.'

'Good.'

'Good? Where's your compassion? Those men are your *friends,* aren't they?

'Only one chief, Neilson.'

'But they're *all* your shipmates. Do you want them shot?'

'Only one chief, Neilson.'

'He'll fire *indiscriminately*… they'll *all* be killed.'

'Good.'

Hercules Duff had had enough.

'*Get off the bridge at once!*' he ordered. '*I'll take the wheel'.* His hand moved swiftly for the telegraph, stopping mid-way at McCall's warning.

'If you alter 'er speed chief, I'll tell the Old Man, an' when 'e's through shootin' them, 'e'll be up 'ere for you.'

'Look McCall,' came the exasperated plea, 'are you perfectly *sane*? What is it you *want*?' Oddball's eyes glowed with malicious madness.

'Ram 'em chief, I wanna ram 'em, I wanna ram 'em, I wanna ram 'em.'

Lifting hands to his disbelieving face, the mate lapsed into thoughtful silence.

'Tell you what,' he suggested at last, 'we'll keep the ship out of range until he's used all his ammunition, then you can ram the lifeboat… Okay?'

McCall was ecstatic. 'And the meat chief?' he asked breathlessly. 'Can I 'ave the chunks o' raw meat from the galley?'

'What chunks of…?'

'To attract the sharks chief. They can smell it a mile…'

'GET OFF THIS WHEEL IMMEDIATELY!'

'I'll tell the Old Man.'

'TELL WHO THE BLOODY HELL YOU LIKE!' This time his face went down to meet his hands. Oh the shame of it. This was the second time he'd sworn this trip.

'Now look McCall,' he began, in quiet composure, but got no further as the Old Man began blasting away and he dived for the telegraph.

Pleased to put the weapon to some worthy use, and hoping Angus McKenzie was taking quivering note, the vessel's reduced speed did not occur to him until he could fire no more. He then ran, hot-foot and fuming, for the bridge. His approach was being closely monitored however, and 'Full Ahead' implemented before his arrival.

None of the shots had any hope of reaching their target – he had never fired a weapon in his life – but this provided no comfort for the terrified men lying prone in the bottom of the lifeboat. Silence had reigned for a full sixty seconds before Neilson raised fearful eyes for a recce. And there it was – the comparatively towering rusted bows of the newly named *Susan Shite* unstoppably bearing down menacingly upon them.

Stand-By

On the east coast of equatorial Africa, where even the chickens seek shade to avoid being barbecued on their feet, lies Mombasa. Peaceful (at least for now), unhurried – a welcoming community in which 'Jambo' is the oft' used friendly greeting. A sun-soaked haven of both calmness and bustle. This is the tropical paradise of multi-coloured travel brochures and multi-coloured dreams. Hugged protectively by jungle, she peeps out across the Indian Ocean – a place for either exploring or recuperation, a kaleidoscope of native culture and crafts to be viewed, admired and, hopefully, bought.

Stretch out beneath the palms and taste of fruits exotica – mango, melon, lime or coconut – best eaten straight from the bough. As you contentedly lounge, disinclined to move, drinking in and savouring nature's bountiful extravagance, innumerable carnivorous insects will be drinking in and savouring *you.*

Beyond the town, narrow tracks wind through villages that have remained unchanged for centuries – their inhabitants carving and weaving goods for market. Bare-breasted women shuffle barefoot, a pitcher of water swaying, unsupported by hand, to a silent rhythm on high, proud, weary yet noble heads. Downstream, mothers with laughing splashing children, still unaware of the raw deal life has allotted them, crouch on the bank, tossing and bashing garments on the rocks. Thus laundered, they too ride home neatly bundled upon heads.

'Er... chippie!' said the Old Man, coming across the boat deck to where the carpenter, stripped to the waist, was working. 'How's the boat coming along?'

The ramming in the Red Sea, although violent enough to

hurl men into the water, had not caught the craft beam-on. Bow collided with bow, spinning the clinker-built lifeboat around to scrape along the side of the vessel, damaging the craft but not sufficient to sink her.

'Fine Cap'n,' the chippie replied, indicating the repairs he'd been making. He said no more by way of explanation or anything else, convinced the Old Man was, like Morgan, a suitable case for treatment, ever since being told to remove his wardrobe mirror and dump it overboard.

'Mmmmm,' the Old Man murmured, and wandered off again.

Refuelling in Aden had been much delayed for the shore authorities insisted that the bunkering berth was booked for a *Susan Snide* and no *Susan Shite* was going to jump the queue.

Glad to be in Mombasa at last, the crew were eating lunch, or as much as their depleted appetites in the 100° plus Fahrenheit heat would allow. Black Eye McKay pulled up his teeshirt and wiped his armpits.

'If the Old Man don't give us a sub t'day, 'e's lower than a submarine shit'ouse,' he sighed.

'Wot can we sell?' asked Oddball McCall, and Neilson shrugged.

'Dunno, unless we can knock off some cargo.'

'There's always the bed linen,' suggested Drunken Duncan. 'We should get a few drinks for that.'

'Don't you ever think of anythin' but *booze*?' sneered Hambone Harrison, who himself thought of little else. 'I mean... don't *women* ever enter y' 'ead?'

'Er... sometimes, but I got a reputation t' consider. If word got aroun' that I'd not spent all my time ashore on the piss, I'd never be able t' lift my 'ead up in Custom 'ouse again.'

'Oh yeah?' sneered Harrison, 'Ah've seen your fuckin' thick 'ead in Custom 'ouse an' y' never *able* t' lift the bastard up.'

'Too bloody right,' agreed the Treacle Bender. 'It's forever slumped over a table in the 'Stepps' or the 'Railway' or the 'Freemasons!'

'There y'*are* then,' cried Duncan triumphantly. 'Wot d'I *tell* ya?'

Big Deal McNiel stared absently into space, his meal of covered wagon (pasty) and chips forgotten on the table before him.

'Ah c'n see 'em all now,' he said dreamily, with slow deliberation, picking his words with poetic care. 'The full length of the 'Anchor Bar'... glass after beautiful glass of ice cold beer, each coated in frosty condensation... the sort that sticks t' y' palms...'

The mess had become a haven of reverent silence: a dropped pin would have clattered like a fallen girder. The image being captured and hugged behind each glazed eye as he went on softly... 'Y' reach for one... y' shirt clingin'... y' pants stuck t' y' fuckin' bollocks... y' hold the glass... admirin' the froth-coated, amber clearness. Then... t' dry, parched lips, y' raise an'...'

'*Stop you bastard. STOP!*' came a distressed strangled cry. 'I don' wanna 'ear about bars lined wi' glass after glass o' beer in frost condensation... so cold it sticks t' y' palm... and certainly not about liftin' 'em to dry, parched lips an'...'

'*Stop you bastard! STOP!*' The Snot Gobbler could take no more, neither could McNiel who said so as he shook his head, eyes painfully closed, only for Duncan to protest.

'But it was your *story*, you prick.' Just then a visitor entered the mess. He was European and when he spoke, he was quite plainly English.

'Morning boys,' he heartily announced.

'Who the hell are you?' a suspicious Nervous Purvis asked.

'Oh someone after your blood,' he said, pinning something on the notice board. He turned back to Purvis who was no longer there.

'Wot y' mean?' asked the Treacle Bender.

'I'm from the local hospital... We need donors,' he explained, 'and as we've always had a good response from merchant seamen...' He shrugged as they exchanged disinterested glances which became wider-eyed in heads nodding with enthusiastic agreement when he added… 'There'll be a couple of beers in it for you afterwards.' He left a mess room buzzing with eager would-be donors.

In response to the appeal, the officers had nominated their most junior, the fifth engineer, to donate a pint on behalf of each of them. He was also to convey their good wishes to the nursing staff with invitations to a shipboard party in their honour the next evening.

On the following morning, seated around the saloon table at breakfast, minus Angus McKenzie and Hercules Duff, they chatted like squirrels anticipating a bumper nut yield when, to their sad surprise, the Old Man entered, grunting like a sow in labour and eased himself into his chair which had remained empty since Aden.

He had been in the grip of a tremulous illness which had included implausible visitations, including hoards of little green men and snakes. They hung around for days terrifying him. Various drugs had been administered, some with extreme difficulty, by Chewsday, who was not without experience having served almost a year in the Royal Army Medical Corps before being discharged from a livelihood he enjoyed tremendously – 'psychiatric grounds' being the dubious terminology.

'Nice to see you up and about again sir,' someone ventured, but no reply was forthcoming.

He knew full well that it wasn't nice to see him up and about again. He ordered a small portion of fish and settled back, glumly surveying the faces glumly surveying him. Hercules Duff arrived and even before he'd taken his seat, the Old Man addressed him.

'There is a notice in the smoke room requesting blood donors.'

'Yes sir, I've seen it. There's another in the crew's mess.'

'Have you a list of volunteers?'

'Not as yet.'

'Then compile one.' The chief mate was feeling hungry

and had been anticipating breakfast but duly rose to leave, snatching a currant scone – which were actually Ayrab fly scones – from a plate, as he made for the door.

'Mr Duff!' the Old Man called after him, 'where in blazes are you going?'

'To compile the...'

'I didn't mean do it *now!* And not personally. You're the chief *officer*. Delegate man! Delegate! Now come and have your blasted breakfast.'

By lunchtime the list was in the Old Man's hands and he proudly beamed around the table, after the list's amazed scrutiny.

'Gentlemen,' he announced, 'this is quite outstanding!'

'Isn't it just, sir,' agreed the sparks, pointing his fork at the lunch before him. 'Mine is quite edible too.'

With a grimace the Old Man went on.

'Every rating has agreed to donate blood. Every last one of 'em. This response must not go unrewarded. Steward! Fetch me a whisky! Now... where was I... Mr Duff?'

'Sir?'

'Notify the men that a payment of five pounds will be issued *after* their return. Not before, mark you. I doubt if they'd get beyond the first bar with it.'

Inflated with self-satisfaction, he poured himself a drink, beaming at all present, then calling for more glasses, he proposed a toast to himself. Angus McKenzie did not participate, having refused the drink and remained seated, permitting himself a contemptuous snigger.

'Ah'd like tae toast ye, right enough,' he muttered to himself. 'In the fuckin' stokehold.'

'Oh, by the way,' the Old Man continued, 'I believe you have the officer's list, Mr Tinkler?'

'Officer's list, sir?' The third mate paled. 'Er... we... it's ... er... we...'

The Old Man passed a weary hand over his face.

'A plain yes or no will suffice.'

'It's... er...'

'Do you have it or not?'

The third mate's eyes darted nervously about, looking in vain for assistance from eyes which averted his, as Angus McKenzie sat, totally detached, viewing the proceedings like one who has had more than a gut full of the liver and bacon which was the day's lunch. The Old Man's voice rose.

'Well? Do I get the officer's list?' With an incantation to the gods, the third mate got slowly to his feet, bringing a sheet of paper to the Old Man before retreating to his chair, with haste.

'WHAT?' came the expected bellow from a face becoming purple with rage. *'ONE VOLUNTEER? JUST ONE* and *HE* a bloody *GREASE MONKEY AT THAT!'*

The fifth engineer cringed. Grease monkey he may be but volunteer – never.

'I'm on watch tonight sir,' offered the third mate hurriedly, 'otherwise you could have counted on me.'

'Good man,' declared the Old Man writing down his name, 'hear that you lot? Any advance on two?'

'B… b… but sir,' stammered the white-faced Mr Tinkler. The mere thought of needles and syringes filled him with indescribable dread, and he was not alone. 'I'm on…'

'Not anymore, you're not. I will stand in for you. Anyway, you'll be back in no time.'

'I suppose y'can put me down, Cap'n,' offered the third engineer, who had no intention of going but wanted this business over with.

'Any more?' asked the Old Man hopefully. Getting no takers, he observed them with disgust. Observing *him* with disgust was Angus McKenzie as he rose to amble out on deck where cargo was being discharged.

'Oh sir,' said the chief steward, coming in from the saloon pantry, taking advantage of the lull, 'I hope I'm not intruding, but…'

'Of course you're bloody intruding Mr Stone, I've never known you do anything else. What is it?'

'A letter, sir. Two in fact.'

'Huh…? Letters…?'

'Yes sir.'

'Put them on my desk,' he instructed. Stanley Stone departed just as a whiff of familiar perfume caught the Old Man's nostrils. He leapt to his feet, eyes asparkle, and skipped after him. 'Where *are* they? Where *are* they? GIMME! GIMME! GIMME!'

Even the galley crew were on the old Bedford boneshaker as it pulled away from the ship.

'Ah hadn't expected *you* two t' be coming,' Hambone Harrison remarked towards the cook and the baker.

'Why not?' the cook replied, 'I want the fiver just as much as you lot.'

'An' my skin might be black,' the baker added, 'but the blood is just the same as yours.'

'Ah'd be fuckin' surprised if it was anything *else*,' agreed Hambone adding sternly, 'But don't go givin' me any o' this racist shite.'

'Nah', he replied, grinning self-consciously.

In all his years on British merchant ships he had never come into contact with views which, ashore in several countries, seemed commonplace. He put that down to the years spent working, eating, socializing and sharing sleeping quarters with others from all over the UK and beyond, leaving an indelible mark. Besides, at the back of each mind is the thought that if they were ever being hauled half-dead into a lifeboat from either rough, calm, freezing or shark-infested waters, they were not going to carp about the accent of the rescuer, the colour of his skin or whether he was straight, bent or a 'twin-screw job'.

''Ow far *is* this bleeding blood bank anyway?' the baker enquired.

'Oh!' cried the Snot Gobbler, 'I *like* it! I *like* it! Bleeding blood bank… Gettit?' The Gobbler had actually been married once. It didn't last long, only until she learned that he was merely an assistant steward on merchant ships instead of the roving ambassador in the import/export business which he had lead her to believe he was. In a remote sort of way, he hadn't lied.

'Y'know,' said Suitcase Larson, as the bus rattled onward, 'I was in Fiji, on this deserted beach, walking arm in arm w' this native girl, late one sunny afternoon, the blue south Pacific gently lappin' the shoreline. Set back from the beach was the palm trees and it was under them that we 'ad this lovely shag. Now, for any young man wi' sex on 'is mind, could y' imagine a better scene?'

'No, ah can't,' agreed Blackeye McKay dreamily. 'In fact, it sounds fuckin' perfect.' And even Chewsday, a smile half playing on his lips, was visualizing the scenario.

'That's wot *I* thought,' he continued, 'until I woke up the next mornin' aboard ship. It was as if every flyin' insect in Fiji had dive-bombed my bare arse. There was fuckin' lumps all over it... the bastards.'

'I just 'ope we're not long in gettin' back,' said Big Deal McNiel. The story of the Fiji girl had rekindled a stirring in his loins. 'I need a woman. That's the first thing on my list.'

'Well, if y'can't find one an' y'*that* desperate,' said Mad McPhee, helpfully, 'there's always Chewsday 'ere.' He winked slyly at Chewsday who was grinning.

'Er...no offence Chewsday,' McNiel went on, 'but I never shove shit up a hill without a wheelbarra, an' even then I'd 'ave t'think twice.'

'Chewsday's got a permanent partner,' broke in Suitcase Larson, '...er...a sort of...er...'

'Live-in turd burglar?' queried McPhee. 'Anyway,' he went on, addressing McNiel again, 'if it was *your* shite in the barra I'd be thinkin' more than twice before I wheeled the bastard *downhill*. I've followed you into the bog-'ole an' it's as if a rat 'as climbed up your arse an' died.' And even Chewsday joined in with the resultant sniggering as the bus bounced onwards.

'You're forgettin' the free beer,' the Treacle Bender reminded him.

'Beer don't mix wi' wot I got in mind.'

'Y' mean… y' won't want your *share*?'

'No, I'll have a drink afterwards.'

'Can *I* have it then?' cried Drunken Duncan, adding 'Please?'

'Hey!' called Neilson, looking around the bouncing bus. 'I don't see 'Nervous', and Chewsday explained that he'd remained hidden on board so it would look as though he'd attended the blood bank and, quick as a flash, Duncan exclaimed.

'Wonderful! Fuckin' wonderful! I'll 'ave '*is* share as well!'

And it was left to Chewsday to explain, in words of few syllables, that as Purvis was not with them, but onboard reading a dirty book he bought in the canal called "The Wrinkled Brown Button of Mrs Brown's Bum" he could hardly be allotted beer after donating blood. Duncan hadn't thought of that.

The sun had almost gone leaving a vast glowing arch like a great jungle fire raging inland. The indestructible crickets were tuning untiring legs for another night-long serenade. The perpetually pernicious mosquito, deadly scounge of man and beast, continued to inflict its toxic presence on anything bereft of self-protection.

Those obliged to suffer the austere simplicity of life remained unimpressed by another sunset. Here and there fires crackled warding off the evening chill and marauding insects. Flickering shadows danced across the black doleful faces as their strange mournful chanting drifted with the smoke into the darkening heavens.

II

'On no account must I be disturbed,' barked the Old Man after the departing steward, as he clutched his letters to his breast like a scowling Shylock.

Self doubt was not a known trait, but it was there, beneath his outer dominance. Insecurity, guilt, unworthiness and vulnerability now fought free of their bonds and floated up like bubbles from a scuba diver. They were becoming (to him) a more noticeable facet of his personality and he began to recognize them as symptoms of his ambition to settle down with Beatrice, and a possible hindrance to his very private desire to discover himself sexually. Indeed the confusion caused by his longings was becoming an exacerbating factor in itself.

Nor was time on his side if he wished, as he surely did, to return to the lady, who had already made her hopes plain, a complete – a *whole* – man. He must at least attain a required condition of some sort of psychological masculinity, a belief in himself where no room for doubtful consternation existed. He must strive to overwhelm and subjugate this torturous mental ambiguousness, burying it beneath a crust of confidence, thick and unbreakable, like those on the cook's pies. This must be firmly established and impressed on his very soul, whatever that was.

Oh, if only things had been different in London, with the *Judith Snide*'s chief engineer's wife. If only she had led him slowly, letting him gain some degree of perception. But her animal insatiability, coupled with her panting, moist and musky nakedness, had initially terrified him and the fright of being on the receiving end of such explosive, instantly thrashing lust, had rendered him incapable of the required procrastination. The premature result had therefore been, quite literally, out of his hands. Yet, given the appropriate circumstances, he felt he might have responded in the manner she so blatantly desired. How successfully he didn't know but was heartened by the memory of that unaccountable and seemingly independent activation which, at the time, had been just another disconcerting addition to his problems, and an acutely embarrassing one at that. Still, it was no use crying over spilt milk.

'Did you *hear* it?' enquired an appropriately concerned Hercules Duff, approaching Angus McKenzie, who viewed, with his usual detached amusement, the colourful spectacle being performed on the main deck below.

'Aye...' he drawled indifferently, '...ah heard.' He allowed himself a thin smile as the elaborate ceremony concluded and the labour force came back on board, apparently satisfied that the banshee-like screams which had rang down from the Old Man's quarters, and had been heard all over the ship, had been banished by the Medicine Man.

Actually they had stopped believing in witchdoctors years ago but still used them as a ploy to take a break whenever the chance arose and the Old Man's cry had provided the perfect opportunity for the vessel to be rendered free of evil spirits.

'You don't suppose...' continued the mate, frowning worriedly, 'that the little green men are back?'

'Ye reckon?' chuckled Angus, hoping so. It would mean, at the very least, protracted incarceration in his quarters and at best a lengthy stay in hospital, out of everyone's way. Mr Duff shook his head sadly.

'I'm afraid,' he said, 'that appears to be the most likely explanation.'

'Yeah... ye could be right at that,' came the dreamy reply, as he nodded in wistful speculation.

'We must call a doctor.'

'Aw... dinna fret yersel, mon.'

'But he needs treatment.'

'Och, aye. He does... right enough.'

'Then, we must...'

'Just leave it tae me... Ah'll see tae it.'

'You'll call a doctor?'

'Who else?' came the innocent reply.

* * *

'*Jambo, Bwana!*' came the loud excited cry as he sprang athletically through the open door, bristling with feathered finery and landing in a perfectly executed splits position on the deck of the Old Man's dayroom. Painted arms were flung wide as he stared dramatically at the deckhead. (Ships don't have ceilings.)

'Jambo' greeted the Old Man in return, not lifting his gaze from the pages in his hand, the ones he was reading with undiminished eagerness for the umpteenth time. The wild screams of delight had subsided into a series of recurring chuckles, head slowly shaking in blissful wonder. Joyfully shed tears lay on his glowing cheeks.

Oh how he'd tormented himself over the possibility of losing his Beatrice to another when, all the while, Sam had been incapacitated with a broken leg, and arm to match. That, he thought, should put him out of the running for quite some time. Sensing a presence, he raised his head, seeing the brash intruder still posed, as if awaiting the curtain's fall, and gave a start.

'Are you for *real?*' he asked, and the figure nodded solemnly.

'Me,' he said, stabbing a finger at his colourful chest, 'man of many medicines.'

'A doctor?' The brightly adorned head nodded aloofly, before speaking, this time in cultured English.

'Instant spells cast, hair grown anywhere, seduction made easy, potency restored, accurate predictions made, sex change a speciality.' He plunged a hand into ruffled feathers and flicked something onto the desk. 'My card,' he murmured condescendingly, as the Old Man scanned it with growing interest.

'You,' he began uncertainly, '…can actually cast spells?'

'Indeed so, bwana,' came the emphatic reply.

'*Real* spells?'

'What other kind are there?'

'I mean… spells that *work*?'

'Of course.' Any annoyance went unnoticed as the Old Man pressed on.

'Real live spells on real live people.'

'*And* animals.'

'In a far away place?'

'Yes. Naturally I would require certain advance details…

name of patient... location... that sort of thing.'

'Of course... naturally,' agreed the Old Man, deep in thought. He stood up and came around the desk, indicating a chair. His smile was warm and welcoming. 'Pray be seated, Doctor. Pull up a nest and sit down. Ha ha ha.'

'Thank you, bwana,' replied his guest, willingly obliging, and the Old Man added.

'Er... I think we can... er... drop this... er... bwana business.'

'As you wish, Captain.' At that he received a knowing wink from the Old Man.

'Er... care for a snort of the old... er... firewater?' he said with a chuckle.

The witchdoctor beamed and generous measures were poured. Returning to his chair, the Old Man launched into a brief explanation of his situation.

'I take it then, Captain, that you require this fellow Sam out of the way?'

'If you could manage it... I mean... he's been taking her *out!*'

'An extended holiday, perhaps?'

'Mmmmm.' The Old Man's brow knit. 'I'm not altogether sure that would suffice. She might accompany him.'

'You know Captain, you are worrying too much. Why don't you just let *her* sort things out?'

'But... what if she doesn't *want* to? Supposing she's grown to like him...' he gave a shudder, '...even *love* him?' His groaning face sank despairingly into his hands.

'That's extremely unlikely.'

'Why?' he asked, through his fingers.

'Well... he didn't sustain his injuries accidentally.'

The Old Man's head jerked up.

'The letter says he fell downstairs. Then how...?'

'He was pushed.'

'Pushed?'

'Indeed... Beatrice had mistaken him for a D.H.S.S. official. I believe she refers to them as spies.'

'The D.H.S.S...? Spies...? But why...?'

'Why not?'

Unable to find a reply, the Old Man got up and replenished the glasses, grinning stupidly.

'So you see Captain, I don't think you need worry.'

'All the same,' the Old Man said thoughtfully, 'I'd be a lot happier if he were far away from her.'

'But is he not travelling to Canada?' The doctor's eyes twinkled merrily. 'Is that not far enough?'

'Yes but...'

The Old Man was about to say that this venture was now postponed until Sam's full recovery, but instead gazed in astonishment at his visitor. This was *incredible*. How had he known that Sam was a prospective migrant? He had not included this in his information from the letter. He remained transfixed in stunned silence as a smile of comprehension spread across the face before him. So he *was* for real. The Old Man felt privileged, nay... *honoured* to be in the company of one so gifted.

'Mmmmm,' mused the witchdoctor, 'I understand. The venture is now postponed until Sam's full recovery.' The Old Man's expression was now worshipful as he special guest star continued.'But you still wish him removed?'

'Well... er... yes. Who knows, she may take pity on him and start bloody *nursing* him. There's no telling *where that* could lead.'

'I see... well, how about... er... death?'

'Er... don't you... er... think that... might be... er... somewhat extreme? I mean... Christ! I don't even *know* the chap. No... death's too drastic.'

'Are there any suggestions you'd like to make?'

'Well...' The Old Man paused to refill the rapidly draining glasses. The flamboyant luminary had already consumed half a bottle and, like the Old Man, his eyes were glazed.

'You must have one,' he prompted.

'Er... how about... er impotency?'

'He still might try.'

'Blast! You're right!' The Old Man look disheartened. 'How about...' he ventured, 'paralysis from the waist down?'

'That would not affect his blood flow.'

'Oh yes,' the Old Man nodded sadly, 'I see... But we must think of *something*.'

The eyes before him closed in silent reflection and remained so for several minutes. Assuming he had fallen asleep, the Old Man reached tiredly for the bottle when, without warning, his conspicuous colluder leapt to his feet in a burst of inspiration.

'Eureka! Eureka!' he cried excitedly, *'I have it'*

'Have what? Have what?' pleaded the Old Man breathlessly jumping upright, shuddering with wild enthusiasm.

'Oh Captain,' he breathed in efficacious relief, 'this is *epoch making...* a real *humdinger*, even by *my* standards.'

'Yes? Yes?' The Old Man could hardly restrain himself.

'I turn him into a gentleman...'

'You mean who wouldn't take advantage of...?'

'...who loves gentlemen.'

* * *

It was a small cell. They squatted uncomfortably, backs to the wall, trying to doze off. Duncan, the first one to be arrested, had bagged the solitary bench on which he slept noisily. The cook occupied the centre of the bare floor when he attempted to rock himself to sleep on his hump. At 0130 hrs the door was flung open to admit he who was pushed stumbling to fall across the cook.

'Hey, you bastard!' he cried angrily, trying to extricate himself from the dead weight. 'Wot the fuck...?'

'Keep rocking, cook,' came the snarl which froze his veins. He quickly resumed as bid.

'Mmmmmm,' approved the Old Man, promptly falling asleep.

Again it had fallen to Stanley Stone to take charge of the

galley, although he did have the baker to do most of the work while he darkly dwelt on recent events. The Old Man had promised to inflict penalty on, and extract retribution from, the insolent, unreliable and irresponsible cook if improved conduct was not forthcoming. But now his own monstrously diabolical behaviour and subsequent arrest had rendered any such punishment ludicrously out of the running.

The Kenyan authorities' reaction upon chance discovery of that which should have been reported had been understandable, and the Old Man must now face the consequences of his folly. Oh how ashamed was poor Stanley Stone to have the police descend in force upon a British vessel; the greatest humiliation of all being the Old Man, frogmarched down the gangway in drunken protestation. *And* under the humorous mocking gaze of the dockers. NATIVE dockers, mark you, not even bloody WHITE men! Of course, he hastily reminded himself, the baker was black, but that was different – *he* was bloody BRITISH!

Hercules Duff, on the other hand, had been somewhat less perturbed. Jail, he reasoned, was one of the few places on earth without alcohol, so he could languish there for a while. He had no personal interest, he reassured himself, no designs on command. No, it was a Christian thing and would benefit the Old Man no end. He did not covet his neighbour's ship, nor his manservant, nor his maidservant, nor his ox... and most definitely not his *ass*.

That afternoon he had paid the jail a courtesy call and as a result was vilified for leaving the ship to the mercy of the chief engineer and for failing to bring him whisky. He'd returned aboard bemused, having learned that the Old Man had been refused bail and remanded in custody for a week and he knew, even then, there was no guarantee of release. They would be ready to sail by then and couldn't hang around paying harbour dues indefinitely.

Deciding not to dwell upon these concerns until after the party with the nurses, during which he hoped for a little flirtation, maybe more (he was only human), he arrived at his quarters to find such diversion quite unnecessary.

'But I'm Captain Bix, you bastards!' came the regular whine through the observation slot in the cell's steel door. *'I must get back to my ship! Let me out, you bloody gangsters! I could have you all logged a month's…!'*

'Calm down Captain,' came the duty officer's weary voice. 'It's futile to…'

'Calm DOWN? Calm DOWN? How in hell's name do I do THAT? My ship is in the hands of lunatics! I simply must get…!'

'You're goin' nowhere Cap'n.' The duty officer was deliberately sitting out of view. 'So you may as well just…'

'Oh but PLEASE… LISTEN!'

'Sorry Cap'n.'

'But it's absolutely imperative…'

'Will you please be *quiet* Cap'n.' There was an edge creeping into his voice.

'But all my men have been released!' The Old Man's eyes were darting about, endeavouring to locate his jailer.

'So would you had *your* offence have been of a minor…'

'Listen… I'll give you…'

'Do not try bribery Cap'n, or you'll be facing another charge.'

'Oh, but…'

'Sorry Cap'n.'

'You lying wanker!' he screamed, *'you're not sorry at all! You're enjoying it! When was the last time you had someone of MY standing…'* He paused to allow a frustrated sob to escape parched lips and he blindly charged the door with a shoulder already heavily bruised from many previous attempts. He recoiled upon contact, holding the injury and howling in agony. *'Oh, for love of God, mister… let me visit my ship… I'll come back… HONEST I will!'*

'Sorry Cap'n.'

'Stop saying you're bloody sorry!'

'Okay… sorry.'

'Just one tiny visit,' he whined on, ineffectually, tears of exasperation forming in ducts. The shakes had already begun. He badly needed a drink. *She is my responsibility... and her valuable cargo. There are vital medicines bound for South Africa.*'

'Stop wasting your breath.'

'But listen...'

'Not a hope.'

'PLEASE!'

'No.'

'Look! There's a consignment of new *uniforms* for the *Kenyan Police Force...* I'll give you first pick... I'll even get you *promoted!*' Just then the Old Man felt that nothing was beyond his capabilities if only he could get out.

'Cap'n,' drawled the considered reply, 'if I let you go free, I'll lose the one I'm wearing now.'

'But have mercy, man!'

'I have my orders.'

'Who do you take them from? The bloody MAFIA?'

Moving with such speed, he hardly caught sight of his face – the observation panel was quickly slid shut with a snap of finality, almost taking the skin from the end of the Old Man's nose.

Back on board party preparations were being concluded and the news that Hercules Duff would not be attending had been gratefully received by all.

'Better off without the Bible-thumping sod,' reasoned the sparks.

'Yeah,' the second engineer agreed, who had a wife back home, but what the eyes don't see... 'He'll probably give us a lecture on loose morals.'

'And besides,' the sparks continued, 'he didn't chip in for the booze.'

'He's teetotal, that's why,' the third engineer explained.

'We all know that, bonehead,' said the second, 'but the girls will be wantin' a drink, an' he'd have wanted one o' the girls.'

'Just because y' got an extra gold braid on y' shoulder

don' give you the right t' call me bonehead...' He paused for thought, then added... 'not outside the engine- room anyway.'

'Well, he's got his arms full right now,' said the sparks.

The smokeroom was unusually decorative, hung with bunting and balloons. There were clean, crisp sheets on each anticipating bunk. Each cabin deckhead light had been thoughtfully removed. The cabins, liberally doused with aftershave, smelled invitingly fresh. There was drink in abundance and, of course, the hosts themselves shone in clean, crisp, tropical white shirts over clean, crisp newly ironed shorts over clean, crisp, aftershave-sprinkled underpants. Pubic hairs bristled in happy expectancy as all present languidly lounged over a pre-party drink, grinning foolishly at one another. Soft sensual music came from the spark's tape recorder. Things could not have been more ready.

'I've heard he's a wardrobe drinker,' said the fourth mate.

'Who?' enquired Cornelius Tinkler, who, although also married, realized that animal instincts override everything, and that a standing cock knows no conscience whatsoever.

'Hercules-bloody-Duff, the guy we were discussin'.'

'Well, I think I know of *one* thing he doesn't do in a wardrobe judging by all the pants and moans and squeals and grunts I heard coming from his cabin this afternoon.'

'Oh!' exclaimed the sparks. 'So he's not queer after all? Are you sure it was a *woman* he had in there?'

As the chuckles died away, the second engineer was inwardly smiling. With the chief mate otherwise engaged, he would be the only one present with three gold braids on his shoulder – advantageous indeed when it came to impressing the ladies. 'Yeah...' he dreamily drawled, half to himself, 'we don't need that sanctimonious sod.'

'Wassa time?' asked the third engineer, quickly withdrawing his hand from a pocket of his shorts, where it had been idly fondling. Before anyone could reply, the sparks, who'd gone out on deck, came running back in.

'They're *coming!* They're *coming!*'

All were quickly standing in bright, wide-eyed unison,

atop the gangway, very aware of how much they had missed female company. They watched, somewhat dazedly, as the coach, with the setting sun reflecting from its tinted windows, crept along the quayside 'twixt piles of cargo. Nervously stroking their carefully groomed hair, they stood at welcoming reception, aching with ill-concealed lust. Their yearning hearts thumped wildly as the vehicle came to a halt.

The door opened and a nurse alighted, a brown-skinned vision of youthful beauty. She smiled and waved in greeting, followed by another of European origin, then a petite charmer filled, or so it seamed to them, with sensual Eastern promise.

'Hi there!' one of them called, shattering the reverie and, in an instant, the gangway reverberated under scampering legs. The nurses were mentally undressed on the spot as introductions were made. After all, these were not pictures in some magazine, but the genuine article – rosy lips, smooth gentle arms, firm rounded breasts, supple waists, soft, yielding buttocks and legs that went right up to... Gulping, in dry-throated wonderment, the sparks found voice first.

'Hi,' he said, 'glad you could all make it.'

'It was sweet of you to invite us all,' thanked the Asian nurse through an engaging smile. His heart almost missed a beat as she gently squeezed a trembling hand. 'It's just what they need to blow the hospital cobwebs off them.'

'Oh, they'll get a blow-through all right,' answered the sparks breathlessly.

'Okay then,' announced the European nurse in business-like manner. 'Shall we get started?' Her blue eyes shone with a mixture of gratitude and pleasure when they nodded enthusiastically. 'Come along then boys,' she called back as she re-boarded the bus. They looked on in bafflement. 'We need some big strong men.'

Blankly they stared at one another. 'Come along boys,' she continued, 'don't be shy. They're your guests and are looking forward to meeting you.'

They stared, gaping in dismay, blood quickly draining from jaw-dropping faces as the first of the happy geriatric patients was helped from the bus. Some without arms, breasts, waists and legs that went anywhere. Dribbling lips were laughing and chattering through toothless grins directed at their astonished, thunderstruck benefactors and hosts for the evening, who were frozen to the spot as involuntary rivulets of urine ran down bare, white-socked, horrified legs which threatened to fold beneath them.

* * *

Deciding that to remain on board was no longer desirable, in light of his unexpectedly altered circumstances, Hercules Duff had booked a double room at the 'White Sands Hotel' away from the expected clamorous shipboard party now viewed as unwelcome distraction. He awoke early, with problems put on hold since her arrival, and lay in ponderance while she slept blissfully on. In the afterglow his mind worked with a relevance, a clarity and a sense of purpose it had previously lacked.

Oh what a fool he had been. The Old Man's machine gun could easily have been dropped into the Indian Ocean during his period of hallucination and he would not have been any the wiser. Customs officers had discovered it hidden under his bed and, not unnaturally, operated under the assumption that where there was one, there were two and so on. After tearing the vessel apart in a quest to find evidence of imported revolution, including the cases of brandy, during which they'd all got very drunk, they found nothing else but decided to impound the ship anyway.

The unenviable task of informing London of the situation now fell to Hercules Duff, who held off, for fear of the Old Man, career in tatters, following him to the ends of the earth in search of vengeful retribution.

'Mmmmmm,' she murmured contentedly, stirring beside him and nuzzling closer as he, guessing that she may not be as emotionally slaked as himself and in need of further demonstration of devotion – brought to a halt by mutual exhaustion – sprang from the bed and dressed hurriedly. There was much to do.

The wedding would take place in Durban – she would sail with them that far, followed by a short honeymoon in the Transvaal. But if the Old Man wasn't released, he would have to assume command. Then London *must* be informed. He was mentally prepared for most eventualities, but not for finding the crew all on board and hard at work. Even the cook had reluctantly resumed duties, although seething with anger and humiliation – pride injured by ungrateful shipmates who had devoured breakfast in jail with exaggerated relish, leaving him in no doubt it was preferable to anything *he* could prepare.

The Old Man paced his lonely cell, having bawled himself hoarse. The officer who had brought him his evening meal, had left with it streaming down his bemused face. Pen and paper had been requested and provided but his letters to Beatrice remained unwritten. How could he send her heart aflutter, inducing in her a craving for him, assuring her of his immortal love with such beautiful prose that the written word itself would send her into paroxysms of masturbatory abandonment. How could he achieve this or anything like, from the abominable surrounding of a jail cell.

Fearfully he paced, conscious of what could happen soon if he didn't get a drink. Everything had been tried – bribery, threat, coercion, nothing worked. Hercules Duff had not been back which did nothing to allay anxieties about the vessel's safety. Robert *had* been right about him after all.

It was getting late and his aching legs sought respite on the hard bench on which he lay, choking back tears. Through the depths of his depression, he suddenly detected movement at the barred aperture in the opposite wall. He shut his eyes tightly against the return of his little green tormentors. When he opened them again, he gave a gasp, his hand stifling a cry.

'What... the...?'

Bejewelled fingers gripped the bars through which a black and white smile dazzled.

'Shhhhhh Captain,' came the hushed reply, and the Old

Man pinched himself.

'Oh,' he sighed at last, 'you're just the fellow I…'

'Shhhhhh.'

The Old Man fell silent.

'Listen carefully, there is not much time. You must sail as soon as possible.'

'But…'

'Shhhhh. Listen. Beatrice has been re-admitted to Tooting Bec.'

'Tooting Bec…? But what's that?'

'A hospital.'

'But… *re*-admitted?'

'Never mind that now. The fact is she was admitted under a section of the Mental Health act which could keep her there indefinitely.'

'I had no idea that…'

'She is.'

'Is she still seeing…?'

'Sam? Forget him. Only her father visits.'

'Good.'

The Old Man was so uptight, his relieved sigh was indistinguishable.

'You've got to get me *out* of here,' he pleaded, convinced that the thousands of miles between them was the root cause of Beatrice's problems. A protective mask was squeezed through the bars to fall on the floor below.

'Put it on quickly,' he was ordered, 'and stand by the door shouting 'FIRE!'

The smoke canister clattered onto the stone floor. The face winked a knowing wink and was gone.

Half Ahead

Sniggering evilly and feeling every inch a prime minister re-
shuffling his cabinet, Angus McKenzie reclined regally,
daintily sipping gin and tonic, little finger raised, reflecting on
decisions a natural leader like him took in his stride. As the
only commodore left on board, he was the unquestionable El
Supremo and certain decrees must be made. Hercules Duff, for
instance – he would assume all navigational responsibilities as
he should because the fellow was a navigator, albeit not a very
good one. The second engineer would become acting chief,
relieving him of any obligation to descend into the engine-
room, whatever the reason. The second cook and baker would
swap with the chief steward. Yes… it was all falling into place.
Stanley Stone as a galley subordinate should greatly please the
cook who would then have no call to subject his meals to
revolting additives. He looked up haughtily as the door
opened.

'Oh!' Stanley Stone exclaimed, 'didn't mean to disturb
you, Mr McKenzie… Everything all right?'

The supercilious commodore glared at him, snapping, 'An'
why *shouldna* everythin' be all right?'

'Well, I thought… as you hadn't dined in the saloon today,
I'd see if you were okay.'

'Ah'm no hungry.'

'Very well, but at sea you rarely miss a meal.'

'Have we sailed?' he asked, sitting upright, somewhat
surprised.

'Yes.'

'Mmmmmm.' This was serious. His eyes darkened as he
flopped back, grimly considering such defiance. For putting to
sea without his authority he would log Hercules Duff one

week's wages... no... make it ten. He focused once more on Stanley Stone. 'Steward...' he snarled, then with a spiteful smile, added, 'or should ah call ye baker?'

'Er... baker, chief?' His brow knit in perplexity and the languid engineer sniggered callously.

'Ye'll be informed in due course. Meanwhile... I dinna need ya concern for mah well-bein'... *especially now*... in *fact*, Stone...' he paused to leer triumphantly at the injured surprise. Even the Old Man addressed him as *Mr* Stone, or steward '...ah'd say ye're attemptin' to curry favour wi' y' betters, ye sniverlin'twat.'

'But... I...'

'Nay use denyin' it. Ye may have fooled that brainless bastard, Bix, but *ah'm* no him. Ye can grovel all ye like but there'll be changes made. Ye're all under new management, an' it's inflexible.'

The steward's mouth opened to speak.

'Dinna interrupt!' came the snapped order, as he looked on in astonished trepidation. I mean... what was *happening* here?

'Mind ye,' the engineer added, after some thought, 'ah'll no be expectin' ye tae bow or anythin' like that. Ye will also address me as Commodore or Sir... I dinna care which.'

'But...'

'Nae more.' Angus McKenzie flicked a limp wrist in Caesar-like dismissal and the steward backed away, mewling under icy tartan scrutiny, to be sent in staggering sprawl by the Old Man charging through the door with a mixture of heartfelt and resented appreciation.

* * *

His cries of 'FIRE!' had brought a swift response from the duty officer who quickly appeared with an extinguisher, only to be rendered unconscious by fumes from the canister. Not a moment was lost. The Old Man was out, discarding the mask as he ran to hail a taxi. He arrived to find the custom guard in spellbound sleep at his post and clambered aboard as silently as he could.

Once on deck, his heart and hopes soared. How stupendously fortunate was he to be blessed with the resourceful, astute Hercules Duff who had, with almost clairvoyant foresight, cancelled all shore leave – to get this far and find the ship deserted would have been catastrophic. Suffused with relief, he marvelled at his first mate's stupendous qualities. How could he have believed Robert for one minute? The man was a lying toe-rag.

He hurried in search of the admirable Hercules to whom he owed more than he could ever repay – his elation mixed with shame at being such a confounded idiot. There was no doubt about it – He'd let his normally unclouded reasoning, his logical processes, be contaminated by the mischievous ravings of a stokehold wallah. It was beyond comprehension and quite inexcusable. The dear old *Susan Snide* and all who sailed in her should give eternal thanks for such an irreproachable, upright, reliable officer of unblemished, inestimable value and faultless character and unquestionable ability – a man of honour.

Yet, to his interminable shame, he had swallowed all that the insufferable Robert had fed him, and as a result, *he*, who should have supported the first officer more unshakably than anyone, had failed him miserably. In addition, he had been intolerably, inexcusably ill-mannered and downright beastly towards the poor fellow.

How could he have *believed* such slander... been so *gullible*? Sex maniac indeed... why the man was practically *divine!* Never could he forgive himself for being weak when he should have defended him to the last *breath*. Why... he was no better than Judas. Still, all was not lost on that front. There would be time for him to make amends.

He reached the mate's door, panting hoarsely, wrenching it open he found, also panting hoarsely and grunting like a pig, Hercules Duff frenziedly fornicating with shameless abandon on a shuddering, bouncing bunk with a shuddering, bouncing, gasping, squealing, naked, spread-eagled female.

The ship came abruptly to life, quietness ordered, as men took up their various stations. It would take more time than the Old Man had to raise sufficient steam pressure for a quick getaway but he'd make do with enough to get her moving initially. Big Deal McNiel and Downtown Daley were sent creeping down to the quayside, taking care not to wake the guard, to let go the mooring ropes – hurrying for the gangway before she drifted from reach. With Hardnut Neilson at the helm, the Old Man stood close by, greedily pulling on a bottle and trembling with fear and excitement. The past few days had been the worst in his life.

Silently, she crept out over the dark waters. He wanted no rattling winches disturbing the unsuspecting night. The stern party manually hauled in the mooring rope, sufficiently to clear the surface so as not to foul the screw, where it was made fast and left hanging. The fo'c's'le rope was left to trail along the surface like the leash of a dog broken free. The Treacle Bender had flashed up furnace after furnace as she slid, inconspicuously towards the gap in the harbour lights.

* * *

Why oh why… grieved Hercules Duff to himself… did I not ensure the door was locked? Whatever possessed me to be so slack? He was doing his morning watch on the bridge and dreaded the Old Man's impending visit, hoping he would exercise discretion in the presence of the helmsman. His head shook sadly. Oh deary, deary me he thought. Anyone walking in on him at such a time would have been unfortunate, to say the least… but *THE OLD MAN?* Oh deary, bloody… yes, damn it! Deary bloody deary me!

The dawn heat settled over the Indian Ocean as a slight swell rolled under her keel in the early mist. Soon the sun would glisten and shimmer across its glassy periphery but the new day held no pleasures for him. On the starb'rd wing he yawned and stretched his aching muscles. It was a delicious ache though, like that of jaws having devoured a thick, succulent, juicy steak.

In his bed, she stirred, pulled the single sheet from her naked breasts and stared about. She felt peculiar, not seasick, she quickly told herself, just, well... peculiar. The sight of the calendar, swinging gently on the wardrobe door, nevertheless made her glad that her stomach was empty. Snuggling back beneath the sheet, she tried to sleep but her thoughts kept returning to the previous night's passion. It had been the best yet, and the first on board a ship. Recalling her back-breaking climax, she lay for sometime in a state of semi-consciousness, interrupted at last by a kiss being softly planted on her dry lips.

'Awake darling?' he breathed softly, then turned to comb his hair in the mirror.

'Mmmmmm, what time is it?'

'About quarter past eight.' He then added casually, 'er... the Captain wants to see me. Just thought I'd pop in on you first.'

On his visit to the bridge the Old Man had, fortunately, not made a scene. Hercules looked lovingly down at her. 'You're a little pale darling,' he said, concern evident despite his own impending doom. 'Is there anything I can do?'

'Oh... I'll be fine dear,' she sighed. 'It's just a bit... you know... unfamiliar.'

'It's only a slight swell and shouldn't get any worse,' he assured her as he stood fiddling with his hands. It was a delaying tactic and he knew it. The inevitable loomed large within his mind.

'Ah well,' he said at last, 'I must be off.' He forced a smile on his anxious face and laughed unconvincingly. 'A man's gotta do what a man's gotta do. I'll bring you back some breakfast shortly.'

'No, No.' She held up a hand, envisaging eggs, bacon, sausages, tomatoes and fried bread glistening in a sea of grease. It turned her tummy. 'Please don't bother dear, I'm not hungry.'

'Okay,' with artificial heartiness, he called from the doorway. 'As you say, my sweetest flower in the garden.'

'Oh!' she called after him.

'Yes, my little treasure island.'

'And don't forget to report him to the Captain.'

'Who?'

'That filthy old pervert who spied on us last night.'

* * *

His spectacular evasion of justice, the Old Man decided, had been eclipsed by the mind boggling sight that had greeted him on his return. He had memorised as many of the details as he could and found himself admitting that, in other circumstances, he would have lingered awhile to watch. Now safely as sea again, he could ponder the matter at length. Wonder what she charges, he thought, pouring himself a stiff one and pacing his carpet reflectively. She may even be *free*... a gift from his great friend the witchdoctor, conjured on board for his own personal enjoyment, only that flaming Duff had got to her first. Robert *had* been right about him after all. His face darkened angrily as he heard the knock on his door.

'Well... come in and sit down... you lecherous swine!'

'Y...yes, sir,' came the whispered response, as he dejectedly shuffled forward on quaking legs. He stood by the chair, head bowed and hands behind his back, as if awaiting the noose. As the Old Man poured another drink, even the clink of glass sent shivers down his spine.

'Now,' the Old Man spluttered, after a drink, 'just what have you got to say for yourself?'

The mate sat down, wearily. 'Believe me sir, I can explain everything.'

'*Explain? Explain?* You'd *better* bloody explain... and be quick about it. Just what do you think this *is?* A *brothel?* Why... if the ratings got wind of this, they'll *all* want a bang, and why not? *The first officer*...?' Shaking an enraged finger, he cried, 'We're supposed to be *master mariners*, Mr Duff, *not whore masters!*' Here the Old Man had crossed permitted boundaries and was taken aback by the mate's instant involuntary reaction, who shot to his feet.

'THE LADY YOU ARE SLANDERING SO MALICIOUSLY,' he screamed, bristling with rectitude, making the Old Man's brows shoot up in disbelief, 'IS SOON TO BECOME MY WIFE! SO THERE!' His angry hand landed SLAP on the desk.

The Old Man was nonplussed... lost for words, and more than a little disappointed for he had been harbouring notions of confiscating the lady for himself. Composure regained, he made a dismissive gesture, which was all he could think of doing.

'Robert was right about you.'

'Robert who?'

'You know damned-well and he was right about you.'

'But who's Robert?'

'I was a fool to doubt him. You're a disgrace to...!'

'But why...?

'You're going to *marry* her?'

'And why *not*?'

'Only *ratings* marry whores... *and* only the dumbest of those.'

The Old Man gave a frightened start as Mr Duff vented anger like never before. *'SHE IS NO WHORE!'* he declared, waving a protesting fist in the air. *'SHE IS NO WHORE AND NEVER HAS BEEN!'*

'So, she's a *has* been?'

'She has never been a has been.'

'Then what is a never has been a has been doing on board my ship, at SEA?'

'She is the perfectly respectable widow of the late vicar of my parish and, with or without your blessing, we are going to be married. I have personally known the lady for...' His zeal was beginning to wane. Never in his entire life could he recall such loss of self-control. He suddenly felt ashamed and drained. He sat heavily down... 'many, many years,' he sighed, head drooping, thankful that throughout this tirade no naughty words had crossed his lips, despite the passion. 'It's...

the truth sir,' he murmured, courteousness returning.

The Old Man's mood had taken a battering, not so much by the unexpected tidings but by their delivery. His normally compliant chief mate had never, to his knowledge, experienced such an outburst of ferocity and he had been completely bowled over by it. A clergyman's widow? His fiancée? Of *course*, it made perfect sense... and *he* had insulted her. I mean... if anyone had insulted his sweet beloved Beatrice in such a manner... his heavenly, darling Beatrice, far too irreproachably sweet to... to shit... he needed a drink, but fast.

Hercules Duff, unable to face a second onslaught, was preparing to leave, with or without permission, when the Old Man, filled with contrition, softly asked him to sit down again. The idea of an apology crossed his mind and he helped it on its way. But conciliatory discussion was called for.

'Now,' he said at last, 'do you mind telling me what a woman, a clergyman's widow or no, is doing on my ship. Her presence aboard is illegal and you seem to be responsible.'

'Well sir... it all started when...'

'I do not require a personal history. Be concise, do not digress. I *have* got all day but I've better things to do with it.'

'Right sir,' he continued, feeling much more at ease, for although his remonstrator was characteristically unsympathetic, he appeared to be viewing his predicament with unhoped for tolerance so an abridged version of events was launched into while the Old Man replenished his glass. He ended by admitting that explanations were not necessarily solutions and found himself suggesting that they put back to Mombasa to drop the lady off. 'She could easily fly down to...' he was saying, when the Old Man, deathly pale, leapt to his feet.

'*Put back to MOMBASA?*' he shrieked. '*Are you completely MAD? What kind of a moron do you take me for? Robert was right about you. You're bloody DERANGED! I'm steering clear of Mombasa, Mr Duff... but PERIOD! BLOODY PERIOD!*' He flopped down, panting, and the disconsolate Hercules got up and ambled out, shaking a sorrowful head. In the space of a few moments he had incurred the Old Man's wrath, appeased him, then incurred his wrath again. Maybe Robert *was* right about him after all.

Soon after, the sparks entered with information that sent the Old Man's blood pressure into orbit.

'JESUS CHRIST!' he exclaimed. *'They can't DO it!'*

'Don't shoot the messenger.'

'But the bastards are planning to re-arrest me in Durban!'

'That's the impression I got too, Cap'n.' I received the wire, remember?' He could see the Old Man was deeply reflecting.

Well, the Old Man thought. They are not the only devious bastards around and my freedom is at stake.

'Sparks!'

'Sir?'

'Thank the agent in Mombasa for this vital information.'

'Will do.'

'And get Mr Duff up here pronto!'

When he arrived, hastily stuffing shirt into trousers, the Old Man's ponderance had concluded.

'We will be altering course,' he said.

'A change of orders from London, sir?'

'Er...' Should this be his excuse? No... there was the cargo to consider. 'Not... er... exactly,' he replied. 'Look, I'll be perfectly frank with you, Mr Duff. I have just learned from the sparks that the consignment of Fermodine we have aboard... y'know... that oral contraception stuff, bound for Durban...?'

'Yes?'

'Well... er... apparently it's going to be added secretly to... er... certain foodstuff preferred by the indigenous native population. The idea being to put an end to pro-creativity and ultimately wipe them out.'

'What?' The mate was aghast.

'Not only that,' he went on, 'but I understand that plans are being formulated for the same to be done with certain undesirables among their own ranks.'

'But,' the mate scoffed, 'they're *all* undesirable!'

'Exactly,' agreed the Old Man with renewed enthusiasm. This was going to be easier than he'd anticipated. They both sat and he leaned across the desk, shaking his head in earnest. 'I was never happy about this consignment, y'know.'

'Nor *I* sir,' came the fervent response. 'Nor *I.*' The Old Man allowed himself an inner smile as he visibly relaxed. He'd guessed right. His chief officer was an anti-contraceptive, pro-lifer. You don't have to be Roman Catholic, he well knew.

'Human life is sacrosanct,' he found himself saying, never having ever given it a second's thought.

'It most *certainly* is, sir.'

'Well, we have it in our power... fate has given us the opportunity to strike a blow for mankind.'

'How?'

'Simple...' he winked slyly at the mate who sat transfixed. Striking a blow for mankind was right up his street, as the Old Man well knew '...we dump the whole Goddamned filth into the drink!'

Upon receiving the eager nods of approval, the Old Man smiled broadly. What inspiration! It bordered on genius!

'We make straight for Lourenco Marques, where we discharge the remaining cargo and load for home.'

'I'm all admiration, sir,' said Hercules Duff proudly. Such news was as welcome to him as a vibrator... in wherever it was they were welcome.'

'Right!' announced the Old Man crisply. 'Turn the men to. Offer them a bonus *and* overtime, plus a ten quid cash advance upon arrival.'

From one wing of the bridge to the other strode the Old Man as his orders were being carried out under close scrutiny. The seas to the stern were a mass of bobbing cardboard cases. There was only one snag. They could not return to the U.K. via the Suez Canal, a route which would take them too close to Mombasa. So they'd round the Cape instead.

It was then that Stanley Stone had appeared, concerned that the chief engineer had not been seen since their departure, and saying that he was going to investigate. After a few moments, this news began to unsettle the Old Man who recalled his infamous treatment of crazy old Angus, without whom, he had since learned, he would never have met his life-saving ally, the witchdoctor. Then there was the engine's response, allowing his pilot-less flight from Mombasa. He couldn't discount that. He owed him much thanks and would hurry to him without delay with a mixture of heartfelt and resented appreciation.

II

It was early evening when the *Susan Snide* berthed at the Portuguese East African town of Lourenco Marques. The promised advanced was issued with the warning that should word of certain unauthorised activities leak, every crew member would be logged the same amount. Apart from the duty watches, a couple of officers and the rats (even Froggy had gone ashore), the vessel was soon deserted. Hardly had the gangway cleared when the padre from the Seaman's Mission arrived to welcome them. He had almost collided with Hercules Duff outside the chief steward's quarters where he had directed a ship's chandler, firmly touting for business. The face of the mate lit up instantly and he greeted the stiff-collared visitor with wild enthusiasm.

'Padre! Padre! Padre!' he exclaimed, beaming as he vigorously pumped his astonished arm. 'Hello! Hello! Welcome aboard my dear Reverend!'

The padre had experienced many diverse welcomes in his missionary career but never one quite as enthusiastic as this. He merely inclined his head, smiling forcibly, as the mate now fondly hugging his tense, alarmed torso, gushed, 'Why, you are the very gentleman I wanted to see.' Taking a step back, hands still firmly gripping the padre's shoulders, he asked, eyes wide with pleasure, 'I trust you are well?'

'Oh... er... so so...' he nodded, pouting sceptically and eyeing the gleeful mate with growing unease. 'I'm... er... not exactly over burdened with work at the moment... er... in fact I...'

'Wonderful!' came the ecstatic interruption, 'your availability right now is a God-send.' Taking the padre's unwilling arm, he led him towards his own cabin, chattering merrily all the way.

'Yes indeed... a God-send. It would be greatly appreciated if you... my dear, dear padre, if you would honour us by conducting a service.'

The padre stopped dead forcing the mate to lose his grip. Removing his spectacles, he wiped them absently with a handkerchief, brow furrowed over suspicious eyes. Was he being made fun of?

'Your... er...' he probed, 'ship's company is religious?'

The mate burst into peals of laughter as on they walked.

'Deary, deary me,' he chuckled, 'no, no... nothing as startling as that.'

The glasses were restored to the padre's smiling, reassured face and Mr Duff continued.

'No, Reverend. I speak of holy matrimony – myself and my beloved.' He paused momentarily, scanning the surprised face beside him. 'Will you do it?'

'But, of *course!*' agreed the padre, without hesitation, then instantly found himself regretting it. A fearful shudder ran down his trembling spine. *Christ!* His eyes closed painfully. Whatever possessed him to *agree* to such...? *His* parishioners didn't live in cosy cottages... roses 'round the door... tea on the lawn. They lived on *ships* at *sea!* Where there were only *men!* His glasses received another nervous wipe as the blood drained from his already white face. 'She... er...' he stammered, faintly moistening lips with drying tongue and swallowing hard, '...she... er... is here... in Lourenco Marques?'

'Within a few feet, Padre,' came the proud reply. As the inwardly quaking clergyman reached the cabin door, his eyes turned heavenward and he prayed silently.

When Hercules Duff arrived, thirty minutes later, to break

the glad tidings to the Old Man, he too, like the padre, was greeted as a long lost brother. The Old Man had been suffering an extremely boring and very thirsty agent. (Anyone would have bored him just then.) He was desperate for solitude to immerse himself into his latest letter.

'Ah!' he exclaimed heartily, jumping to his feet, gratuitous relief evident in his eyes. 'Come for your revenge, as promised?'

The mate frowned. 'Er... revenge, sir?'

'Yes... it *was* now we arranged to play... wasn't it? He was hastily setting up the chessboard.

'Er... play, sir?' he ventured, and the Old Man shot him a warning glance.

'It was, it was,' he went on. 'Sit down Mr Mate.' Obeying, Hercules sat down but decided to try again.

'Sir... I have...'

'Your move,' hissed the Old Man through a clenched grin.

The mate gave a shrug of helplessness and began. The game proceeded in silence, broken only by an occasional meaningful cough from the agent as he toyed unhappily with an empty glass. Just as the Old Man was beginning to despair of him ever taking the hint, and also just as the chief mate, by now engrossed in the game, was about to checkmate him, the agent gave a curt goodbye and left.

'Right!' exclaimed the relieved Old Man, scooping up the pieces. 'Game over. Stalemate.' Then he delved into his pocket for the envelope at which he feverishly tore. He then glared at the first officer. 'You still here?' he growled. 'The game's over..'

'But sir... I came to tell you...'

'Leave...! Begone...!'

'But...'

'Get t' hell out!'

But Hercules Duff was sticking to his guns.

'I'm getting married tomorrow. Sir. I wish to take some leave.'

The Old Man, oblivious to all but the perfumed written

page, understood not a syllable, growling, 'Yes, yes, yes. Now please leave me alone.'

The mate left in a euphoric daze. He was ever so happy and happy to be happy. He was even happy to be happy to be happy, and you can't get much happier than that.

The reading, over and over again, of his letter had made the Old Man happy too and he embarked upon an immediate reply. He explained how they were loading a cargo of cocoa beans packed in cardboard drums bound for Liverpool, and gave, as best he could, an approximate date of arrival. He hoped she would be there to greet him, in all her exquisitely feminine finery, as she had indicated she would. Nearer the time, he advised her to contact head office for a more detailed docking date. He also added some miscellaneous points of interest, such as brilliantly checkmating the chief mate, the esteem in which he was held by all his subordinates, and Angus McKenzie's hospitalisation.

* * *

Having grudging consented to be best man, never having attended a wedding in his life, his motives were purely selfish. If he himself was also to wed, and such was in the air, he would need to study the ceremony for he had no wish to make a fool of himself abreast of one so dear. He intended to observe the bridegroom closely and take notes.

'Steward!' he barked, entering without warning, just missing the drawer being snapped shut. Stanley Stone had been, like the king in his counting house, counting out his money.

'Sir?' came the alarmed cry, as he bounded to his feet, moving from the bulging drawer.

'Er… about this blasted wedding,' began the Old Man uncertainly, as he sat down without invitation. 'You're going, I suppose?'

'Oh, indeed sir,' came the relieved reply.

'And you, sir?'

'I'm best man, you dunderhead.'

'Oh, yes of course.'

'When *is* the ceremony?

'Twelve noon tomorrow, I believe sir.'

'Mmmmmmm... er... I *was* informed where but I've... er... forgotten.'

'Easily done, sir,' came the obsequious reply.

'Then tell me... *where?*'

'The mission, sir.'

'What about the... er... *do*, afterwards?'

'The reception, sir?'

'Yes.'

'The mission again, sir.'

'Mmmmm.' He lapsed into thought as Stanley awaited patiently. 'Will there be many present?' he asked at last.

'I recall Mr Duff saying that they wished for a quiet affair.'

'What about the... er... honeymoon. Where are they planning to go?'

'I don't know sir... anywhere.'

'Anywhere?'

'Well... yes.'

'Mmmmmm.'

'A safari brochure was seen in Mr Duff's accommodation during cleaning, sir.'

'Safari?' The Old Man closed his eyes and spoke in a strained tone. 'This is one hell of a sized continent, Mr Stone... and, well... anywhere could mean... *any bloody where!* And SAFARI...!'

'Well, yes... I imagine so.'

'They could be gone for days... *Years!*'

'Yes, sir.'

A thought suddenly struck the Old Man. 'Who's paying for all this...? Such a trip could cost a fortune. I'd no idea Mr Duff was wealthy.'

'Oh, but he isn't sir.'

'Then where is the money coming from?'

'Well... sir... it's none of my business but... I believe the bride is footing the bill.'

The Old Man's brow knit. 'Isn't that rather... well... unusual in matrimonial affairs?'

'I really couldn't say, sir,' the steward replied, equally ignorant on the matter. The Old Man was frowning, scratching his chin.

'Steward,' he sighed at last, 'I need a drink.'

So, he thought darkly, Mr Duff's true character emerges. It would seem that Robert *was* right about him, after all. All this lovey dovey business was a load of shite. The greedy bastard was marrying *money!* Well he may marry whomsoever he chooses, but as for a bloody safari...

By the time the steward brought him his drink, the Old Man was actually smiling, albeit maliciously, which was nervously acknowledged.

'What's the time now?' he asked, draining the glass in a single gulp.

'Seven thirty, sir.'

'Mmmmm.' He stood up and began to pace – always a sign. 'Mr Stone?'

'Sir?'

'Type out a notice saying that all hands are invited to the wedding... compliments of the bride. Absentees will be heavily logged.'

'Oh, I say, sir,' the steward gushed, 'that's jolly good of her!'

'Yes, isn't it?' he agreed mischievously. 'Very cordial... Now don't forget to mention unlimited free booze.'

'Very good sir,'

'They can drink themselves senseless. In fact... they *will.* That's an order. Put it down and stick it up in the crew's mess.'

'As you say sir.'

The Old Man strode out purposely, his mind in overdrive. Fifteen minutes later the chief steward was at his door.

'I've done the notice sir, but there's no point in displaying it as there's no one on board to read it.'

'No one at all?' The Old Man could see his best laid plans going the way of mice and men.

'None that I can see sir. Only the second steward in the galley.'

'What's the second doing in...?' He checked himself at once. 'No! No! Don't tell me!'

'I knew what would happen if they got that ten pounds. Even the baker's...'

'Yes, yes,' snapped the Old Man irritably. 'It doesn't really matter. How can they attend the wedding if they don't get time off?'

The steward droned on, aggrieved. 'But that's tomorrow! They should never have given him that company contract.'

'Huh... who...?'

'The cook, sir. Just because he's got a job for life, he thinks he's got a job for life!'

'Will you shut up about the blasted cook, Mr Stone. I'm trying to *think* here.'

Pouring more scotch down his throat and belching, the Old Man resumed his pacing, his mind a hive of activity. The steward looked dolefully on.

'Listen carefully,' he said at last. 'This is important. Copy that notice half a dozen times... no make it two dozen. Then call a taxi and leave a notice in all the local bars and hovels.' He glared at his watch. 'I want it to be seen by all the lads by tomorrow morning. Scour the whole bloody area if needs be. The cab fare goes on the wedding bill.'

'I say, sir, *that's* jolly decent of her!'

'Hop to it man. Time is of the essence.'

* * *

Although a quiet affair had been envisaged, the bride, and especially the groom, who'd had no inkling of his popularity, were touched by the large turn-out. It was an unexpected sign of respect and the heart of Hercules couldn't help but be emotionally affected. It went out to them all in gratitude although the couple were somewhat bemused by the contingent of native girls some of the guests had brought with them. This proved an added bonus for the Old Man.

He'd made his peace with the agent, for he needed his help. Together they had accomplished much in such a short time. Tables stood end to end in the mission hall, laden with bowls of fruit and bottles of wine: cigars abounded and African waiters, immaculate in white tunics, stood to attention awaiting orders. A mobile kitchen was parked outside, next to a refrigerated van full of champagne. After the short solemn ceremony, in which the Old Man excelled, the corks began to pop in earnest with the padre looking on, an unwelcome, indefinable something in the pit of his stomach.

The Old Man gratefully declined to make a speech while the mate sang the praises of all concerned for making the occasion so memorable. The padre then rose to speak and everything mentioned seemed to have religious connotations. He sat down to tumultuous jeering.

'Now, now now!' the Old Man counselled sternly, coming to his feet, an admonishing finger waving to quell the commotion. A hush descended. 'The padre here is absolutely right! I endorse his every word! Why… you ought to be ashamed of yourselves!' He smiled sympathetically at the clergyman who was thanking the Lord for the presence of someone with a semblance of dignity and the power to enforce it. 'So in future… when addressed by a man of the cloth… kindly show some respect. This sordid behaviour does neither you nor the ship, any credit whatsoever… And another thing… Just because the bride is footing the bill for this expensive feast, it's not a open invitation to over-indulge.'

His gaze fell meaningfully in turn, on each present, before continuing. 'But for those who inadvertently do… the lady is providing free transport for anyone doubting his ability to return to the ship unaided.'

He resumed his seat midst deafening cheers as the swooned bride was carried out to make first use of the facility.

'I say sir,' exclaimed Stanley Stone, leaning across the

table. '*That's* jolly good of her.

* * *

Angus McKenzie was well aware that the Old Man hated his living guts, wishing they weren't living at all, long before he'd mistakenly trodden on his balls years before during celebration of his elevation to commodore chief engineer. Apoplectically witnessing the charge into his cabin, however, after being self-convinced of the Old Man being securely left back in Mombasa under lock and key, had him leaping, dumbstruck, to his feet as if seeing a ghost. He'd only half completed the manoeuvre before the head of the sprawling chief steward hit him on the mouth, sending his pipe plunging down his alarmed throat. He collapsed in a breathless gagging heap, head forced back, with only the bowl of the pipe visible between his dentures.

Blood bubbled at his lips as a result of the un-prescribed tonsillectomy. The lymphoid tissued appendages themselves must have been swallowed and digested, for throughout the following days of vomiting, to his disgust, he didn't see them despite close investigation. How fortunate, the Old Man laughingly thought later, that he had been smoking one of his straight-stemmed pipes. No telling what damage the other variety could have caused.

The recuperating engineer was dozing fitfully as he caught the faint sound of the turning doorknob of his private hospital room and was instantly alert. Gaping, he watched as the door was opened with, to him, slow deliberation, revealing the slight figure of Stanley Stone. He relaxed with an audible sigh as his visitor tiptoed in and sat by the bed.

'Hello Mr McKenzie,' he said amicably, 'are you feeling better?'

'Ummmph... Nae better f' seeing *you*. In fact... the more ah see o' ye, the more ah believe in birth control.'

'Now, now, Mr McKenzie,' he chided, in the tone of one holding the trump card, 'are they taking good care of you?'

'What the hell *d'ye* care? Or anybody?'

His sourness was ignored as the steward changed the subject.

'I'll never forget the last time I was in hospital,' he said cheerily. 'Years ago it was. I had an operation on my...'

'Bollocks!' the patient replied, turning to the wall.

'No, no,' tittered the steward. 'My stomach actually.'

'I dinna fuckin' care.'

After giving a delicate cough, he tried again. 'Are you being decently fed?' For days previously the engineer had been unable to eat at all.

'A damned sight better than on the ship,' he snapped, then suddenly he rolled back to face him. 'O' *course,*' he exclaimed, 'that *accounts* for it!'

'For what?'

'For ye havin' nae guts... they were taken oot!'

'Now, Chief... please...'

'Chief, please nothin', ye suck 'ole bastard. The way ye snivel and grovel aroon the Old Man's arse. Yes sir. No sir. Three bags full sir,' he leered, 'ye make me...!'

Stopping abruptly he made a grab for a nearby kidney dish into which he heartily vomited. *'There ye are!'* he declared triumphantly, wiping lips on the back of his hand and pointing dramatically to the steaming liquid. *'What did ah tell ye?* That's *exactly* how ye make me feel!' He thrust out his chest with pride at such perfect timing. Disgusted, Stanley Stone sighed and got up to leave.

'Well... if that's how you feel...'

'That's right, ye prick... GO! Get oot o' mah sight... an' STAY oot...!'

As his rantings subsided he noticed the sly, mocking and extremely disconcerting grin spreading over the face of the steward. Stanley Stone was not in the least disappointed, having fully expected to be thus received. Now he revelled in it for his vengeance would be all the sweeter. Purring contentedly, he turned at the door.

'The Old Man sent you this,' he said, producing an

envelope.

'Oh yeah!' came the suspicious response, 'an' what does *he* want?'

He had to wait some time for a reply as the steward was savouring every second's delay.

'Well?' he snarled, hoping to mask his discomfort. 'What's it aboot then? Ye'll have to read it t' me... I dinna have mah damned glasses.'

'I don't have to,' came the haughty retort. 'I know what it says.'

'Well... What is it, ye bastard?'

The smile on the steward's face grew wider. After yet another spiteful pause, he said,

'Mr Duff was married yesterday.'

'Oh yeah...? And who did *he* marry... the chippie?'

Beaming the steward flicked the letter across the room.

'For failing to attend the wedding... you are hereby logged one month's pay.' He lingered by the door smirking at the nonplussed patient and trying to catch the scene indelibly on his memory. He then wafted away as silently as he'd come.

Slow Ahead

It was yet another morning of mourning. Mr and Mrs Duff had still not yet returned and the two glistening, brown-skinned visitors were soaking up all the booze in sight, as they had for the past four days. The Old Man would not have minded had they succeeded in turning him into something useful to Beatrice. But they had failed... or, rather, he had. In desperation he had even attempted self-enforced sobriety, and to hell with hallucinations, but with his quarters almost permanently ringing with the sound of clinking glasses, this had been in vain. He had even burst into quiet tears in the privacy of his shower... frustration mingling with the suds to gurgle down the scupper in a whirlpool of heartbreak.

He'd just been deluding himself. How could he obtain his heart's desire without co-operation from his body? Poor Beatrice, he thought. Poor, poor, pure Beat... It would never happen now. Their blissful future together was an impossible dream, a mere self-deception, the tactic of a bored, tired mind in search of diversion. Sorrowfully he recalled never having been quite convinced. More like he'd been sidetracked by cruel coincidences, meddling fiendishly with his benighted subconscious.

And yet... in London... with the wife of the *Judith's* chief engineer... Had it happened? Had she been real or had the whole episode been yet more illusion? Had she been from the same plane as his little green men? But what about the stirring and what followed... surely he couldn't have dreamt *that?* His head shook sadly, remembering his elation at the prospect of a new door to life's mysteries about to open... Ah... sweet gullibility.

On express command, no one had approached the Old

Man's door since the reception, so Stanley Stone was somewhat surprised at being summoned. He tapped lightly and, smouldering with curiosity, tried the handle. It was locked.

'Is that you steward?' came the Old Man's voice, followed by a conspiratorial 'Shhhhhh!'

'Yes sir,' he replied, peering through the keyhole, but leaping back instantly as the Old Man's eye blazed back at him.

'I want you to go ashore.'

'Now, sir?'

'Yes. Check out the hotels in town and find out where the mate and his wife are staying. Then report back to me.'

'I think I already know sir.'

'You do? Which is it?'

'The Lisboa.'

There came no reply from beyond the door and the steward, instead of leaving, pressed his ear to it and, with some difficulty distinguished much furtive whispering. Oh what he would give to be able to see... Then, suddenly, without having to give anything, he could... The door had been yanked open with him half stumbling in, giving a shriek of alarm. He was roughly shoved back out by a stark naked Old Man, yelling, *'Carry out my orders at once, you nosey bastard!'*

'But sir... it's the Lisboa.

'Make bloody certain!' He hurriedly left, leaving the Old Man framed in the doorway, appendages quivering with indignation as he shook with rage.

* * *

Oh how foolishly confident he'd been, travelling back from the reception, stroking a moist thigh with each hand, heart pounding with expectation. He'd began stripping upon arrival, panting and gasping while he hopped on one leg, shaking his trousers from the other.

It had been with a shrug of resignation that the two nut-brown maidens, each a genuine virgin in her left ear-hole, did likewise, exchanging glances which clearly indicated, 'Whatever we get off dis bastard we gonna have t' earn.' It became apparent, however, that he needed probably more stimulation than either were capable of providing. He needed... a... a chief engineer's wife... or... at the very least... a demonstration like...

On the off-chance that the honeymooners had returned undetected, he pulled back his carpet and dropped to his knees, ear to the deck, trying to detect sound of habitation in the mate's cabin below. His nubile young guests exchanged understanding nods as smiles creased their pretty faces – mystery solved. At last they knew how to please the Old Man.

The first indication the Old Man got that they knew how to please him was the swish of bamboo parting the air en-route to his inviting cheeky expanse of bare unsuspecting buttocks.

In the Lisboa Hotel next morning, Hercules Duff had awoken, trying to remember the last time he had partaken of a meal. His thoughts were also beginning to turn – for the first time since the wedding – to the ship and his hopes that the second mate, Thorndike Camp, was ensuring cargo was being correctly stowed and the bosun was getting sufficient work from his hands. He was brought abruptly back to the present by her husky voice, in between nibbling his ear. This was no use. It was approaching lunchtime already and he was ravenous. If he didn't eat soon he'd be too weak to... He glanced quickly at his watch, overwhelmed by the need for sustenance and, pulling gently free of her panting grasp, he got up.

'Good morning, my dear,' he greeted the maid in the hall, en-route to the restaurant. He had a strange fancy for oysters, the supposedly aphrodisiac properties of which had been subtly implanted in his mind upon her learning of his hunger.

'Jambo bwana,' came the courteous murmur.

'And t' you, Madam.' Madam gave a condescending nod and they descended the stairs. Immediately the maid entered the room next to theirs, discarding cap and apron and turning into one of the Old Man's girls. 'It okay! It okay!' she whispered. 'Day gone! Day gone!'

'Will day be gone long?' her friend enquired.

'Long enough,' muttered the Old Man, taking a drill from his suitcase and attacking the dividing wall.

The slightly unwilling Mr Duff was led back by his bubbly insatiable bride. The oysters were superb and she had encouraged his abundant indulgence in the slippery little blighters until his stomach contents must have resembled a repleted spittoon.

'Right,' she breathed sensually, locking the door behind her, 'let's find out if the old adage is more than mere myth.'

And indeed it was. He was soon proud and erect. Her very own John Wayne settling in the saddle. She responded with a jerk and whinnying cry as off he rode in hot pursuit, armed to the gonads with millions of hell-bent little what's-its. She groaned and snorted beneath him; fingernails raked his back like spurs demanding more speed. A low moan was heard from another location and he almost tumbled from his bucking charger, but re-focused on the ride in hand. *These Goddarned ornery, besky paddies must be brought to justice.*

The gap was closing now and the distant moaning increased in volume with each thrust. He shook his steaming head, bending over flaring nostrils and dug in harder. It was too late now to turn back and investigate. Hoarse gasps broke from her cavernous mouth as on he mercilessly pursued with tenacity hitherto inexperienced and she whimpered uncontrollably. His quarry's hooves reverberated in his ears. *THERE WAS NO STOPPING NOW! ONE FINAL SPURT!*

'Ohhhhh, Thank you God!' she cried. 'Yes! Yes!' and with a final mutual 'Ahhhhhhh!' they came to a shuddering halt. He collapsed beside her thinking *besky paddies?* As a rapturous, victorious yelp – but not from them – had them sitting bolt upright exchanging a puzzled, sweaty gaze.

* * *

Unworried that a passing breeze might lift him and his unburdened heart up into the stratosphere, the Old Man laughingly escorted the manager of the Lisboa Hotel to the gangway. He then made for the chief steward's cabin. He was, as was plainly evident, a new man – effervescent, magnanimous and quite beguiling. Suddenly he was swaggering around, smiling and greeting all in sight, even the ratings, and calling

'Watch the sun now, Larson, it's blistering today,' and 'Have you any protective lotion, Duncan old chap?'

Never having been convinced that he was totally sane, the crew were now of the opinion that he was away with the fairies, and they weren't far wrong. Nor did his newly acquired magnanimity towards the native dockers, treating each as a blood-brother, go unnoticed. His generous distribution of gifts ensured that there were no more contented stevedores in all Africa than those working the *Susan Snide.* In fact, so unwilling were they for her departure that the cargo piled up on the quayside, instead of in her holds.

Strutting with humorous pride, he even paid a rare visit to the engine room where the firemen were repairing brickwork in the furnaces.

'Take it easy there, fellows!' he called, genuinely concerned. 'Don't want you hurting yourselves just for a silly old boiler, what?'

They readily concurred, but the second engineer, outraged at this intrusion into his domain, snapped. 'The job's gotta be done, Cap'n. They're used to it... Bin doin' it for years... Incapable of anythin' else, y' understand.'

Ignoring the second's mood, and not wishing to be outdone, the Old Man exclaimed, 'Tell you what... I'll send down a couple of cases of ice cold beer...! How's that?'

As the men cheered, the second scowled, thinking it would be a different story if they were obliged to put to sea again without a full head of steam. This intervention had upset him and he never imagined that he'd find himself wishing for the chief's return, but he was, and it was granted.

'*Angus!*' came the ecstatic cry from the main deck where the Old Man stood, arms held wide in a Christ-like pose of welcome. He then came hurrying down the gangway to greet the fearfully startled engineer who backed away as far as the cargo would allow.

'*Keep y' distance, ye bastard!*' he snarled, holding up an arm. He then grabbed a drum of coffee beans which he brandished aloft. '*Dinna come any closer!*' he warned, but the Old Man was offering the hand of friendship as he advanced slowly.

'Angus, my dear, dear chap!' he gushed. 'My trusty compatriot.' Stopping a safe distance from the growling engineer, he just stood there, a picture of contriteness. 'You see before you... Angus...' he said softly but with much emotion, 'an unworthy man. I ask you... Nay! Plead with you for forgiveness! And I'm also so sorry I couldn't come to visit you in hospital but I've been... well... busy.'

'Huh?' came the stunned reply. Was he hearing correctly?

'And oh... Angus!' he continued, every inch a sinner, 'I am filled with remorse about the accident. I was in such a hurry to thank you... *really* I was. I didn't expect Mr Stone to be there, old friend. Believe me, I was absolutely devastated, truly. Ohhh Angus... dear, wonderful fellow that you are, I am despicable... deserving of all your detestation... unfit to share the same ship.'

The raised drum slowly lowered throughout this, quite moving, if unbelievable confession, as also did the jaw of Angus McKenzie. He stared, wide-eyed at the Old Man's sadly shaking head and failed even to blink when the Old Man called for the nearest rating to fetch his gear from the taxi and bring it aboard. He then gently led his numbed body towards the gangway.

'Oh Angus,' he grovelled, 'can you ever find it in your generous heart to forgive me...? Please say you can!'

But he couldn't say anything because he was speechless.

'Heaven knows,' the Old Man wailed on, 'I little deserve it.'

Concussed, the engineer wondered briefly if he had died and gone to that select heaven reserved for commodores. He just sat mute and still, in the Old Man's dayroom, where he'd been led, and dazedly watched the two naked native girls giggling drunkenly. For the first time he was aware how racially portrayed, intentionally or not, centuries of Christian art had been. Not even Michelangelo had ever hinted that angels could be anything other than white. Now it was his turn to feel ashamed that he had never thought of it before.

* * *

'Stanley, me boy!' came the Old Man's hearty greeting, still grinning from the hotel manager's visit. 'Please deliver this book of traveller's cheques to the Lisboa will you?' He didn't order any more... he asked, politely.

'Certainly sir,' the chief steward replied, knowing that no matter how politely he asked, he still expected it done.

'Apparently,' he chortled, 'they find themselves in something of an embarrassing predicament.'

'Really, sir?'

'The wedding bill has arrived and they don't have sufficient funds to meet even the hotel's requirements.' He was chuckling quietly. 'Can't have them washing bloody dishes on their honeymoon, can we?'

'Oh I should say not, sir,' the steward agreed, who himself had been sadly calculating the cost of the Old Man's recent unaccountable philanthropy with the ship's bonded stores. It did not make soothing reading.

'Say I'm frightfully sorry and all that, but I found the cheques at the reception and clean forgot to hand them back. He had found them right enough, in the lady's handbag. They weren't embarking on any damned safari if *he* could prevent it.

'I'm on my way, sir.'

'Oh... and Stan...' he paused thoughtfully, and the steward's eyebrows raised at the informality.

'Sir... anything else?'

'I think... er... you may drop the 'sir' when we're in private... it's too bloody... well... distant, don't you think?'

'Er... yes, sir... I mean...'

'Makes me feel like a bloody tyrant.'

'Oh... I...' the steward dried up and the Old Man spread out his hands appealingly.

'I'm not a bloody tyrant, am I Stan?' he asked.

The steward was beginning to look distinctly uncomfortable, but forced a reassuring smile. 'Oh most certainly not, sir.'

'Now, now Stan,' he chided, 'I said drop the 'sir'.'

'Very well, sir... Oh...!'

'You *do* know my name, Stan?'

'Yes indeed.' He was shuffling nervously.

'Well?'

The unnerved Stanley Stone remained silent. This was one hell of a social jump. To be this informal with the Old Man after so long would not be easy, and what if all this was some kind of perverted gag, or maybe a symptom of an illness?

From the onset of this personality change, the chief steward had trodden warily. Raising eyes, he scrutinized the Old Man whose eyebrows were raised expectantly as he nodded encouragement.

'Come on, Stan... I won't bite you.'

'Er... er... er...'

'Oh come along... surely after all this time... we've known each other for *donkeys!* Come on now... try saying my name.'

The Old Man was grinning happily as the steward swallowed hard. Years of subservience to a ship master whose manner insisted upon it, had not, even fractionally, prepared him for this obligation.

'Er... Craw... Craw...' His bottom lip trembled with dread as he wiped sweaty palms on the seat of his shorts.

'Yes? Yes?' prompted the Old Man, in eager support, and the voice of the quaking steward dropped to a whisper.

'Craw… Craw… *Crawley*,' he squeaked at last, making the Old Man slap his back heartily.

'*There you are!*' he cried. 'It wasn't so bad, was it?' He then winked at the elated steward. 'You old sod!'

The glazed eyes of the steward stared vacantly into space. The Old Man, as always, had been right. It *hadn't* been so bad… in fact it felt… *ever* so good. Heavenly. Squaring his rounded shoulders, determination blasting away all timidity and surging with self-confidence, even bravado, he looked at the Old Man coolly.

'Hello Crawley!' he said and burst out tittering as the Old Man, overcome with such pulverising wit, held his sides, rocking helplessly.

'Now… off you go, Stan…' he managed, eventually. '…Tell 'em to… drop whatever they're doing and…' he nudged the giggling steward meaningfully, '…honeymooners…?' he chuckled, 'drop whatever they're…'

Collapsing into each others' arms, they quivered with unrefined joy, their tears dampening each others' shoulders in the process.

'Oh my… dear me…!' the Old Man gasped, straightening up, dabbing his flushed happy face. 'My… but that was funny.'

'It… it… sure was… *Crawley!*' gasped the steward, which released another flood of giggles. It was some time before the Old Man could continue, shoulders heaving.

'Tell them…' pausing to wipe his swollen eyes, '…that I'm throwing a shipboard party for the bride before she flies home.'

'Aye, aye… Crawley!' responded the steward, by now tottering about, intoxicated with mirth. Suddenly he came smartly to attention, struck by unparalleled inspiration.

'*Aye Aye… Crawley BIX!*'

The unmerciful hilarity was overwhelming and the Old Man staggered into the alleyway, bent double, holding his aching abdomen. He dropped, helplessly to his knees. His streaming eyes turned blindly towards the cabin door to which he crept on all fours. Stanley Stone was holding the frame for support, wracked with merriment. He looked down at the Old Man.

'Don't be... Don't be... *Don't be a CREEPY CRAWLEY!*' came the strangled cry.

'*OH... NO...! NOT... AGAIN...! YOU BAS... BAS... BASTARD!' wheezed the* Old Man, rolling over onto his back, legs in the air. Their unbridled joyous intoxication came in bronchitic-like gasps of breathlessness. 'It was delightful. It was delicious. It was de-lovely.'

'And don't... forget to tell her...' said the convulsive Old Man with intensive effort, as the steward looked away, biting his thumb, '...that this time...' again they both shook and the Old Man pinched his nose and took a deep breath... *'IT'S ON ME!'*

* * *

Although invited, Stanley Stone did not attend the party. Such disgusting gatherings were not for him. The sight and sound of the saloon and smokeroom just then, with its large contingent of happy native girls, joyously mingling with the equally happy officers, wild abandon ready to reign, filled him with disgust. The only relationship he'd ever enjoyed was with money. Unable to sleep, he wandered onto the main deck where the sky blazed with stars and crickets ceaselessly did their stuff.

Mosquitoes and dragonflies twinkled under the cargo cluster lamps shining above him. An occasional bat winged by on its precise way, casting eerie shadows on the warehouse roof opposite. He noticed, with some interest, a praying mantis, statuesquely clinging to a rope. Its almost translucent fragility glistened in the light and he stopped to stare.

He dismissed the idea of going ashore. He rarely did these days, and certainly not at this hour for fear of meeting a drunken deck or engine-room hand, with his infernal, wearisome complaints – they were all insufferable and the silly, childish officers, not much better.

He saw deck officers believing, almost to a man, that a vessel's safety and that of her crew and cargo and, therefore, the nation's welfare, depended entirely on their navigational skills; secretly yearning for the old days of sail, with engineers ashore where they belonged, reinstating them to their rightful positions of total power. Though, for many, the sailing of a ten foot dingy would present insurmountable problems.

He saw engineers united in the belief that a vessel's safety depended entirely upon their mastery of all things mechanical. As they longed for the day when navigation would depend upon highly sophisticated technology, and only engineers would be entrusted with ships at sea. Though, for many, the mechanics of the pedal bin were far from grasped.

To Stanley Stone, each officer of either department was lacking even the combined brainpower of the audience of a TV group therapy session masquerading under studio debate.

'Hi, Mr Stone!' He turned to see the sparks, happily arm in arm with one of the party girls, taking in the night air. From him he then learned what the officers already knew. The elation he'd felt at finally being elevated, in the Old Man's eyes anyway, to a degree of equality – first name terms and all that – vanished at the news.

Sir Vyvyn K had married a long-time Asian friend and business acquaintance, Mr Chung Fu, owner of one of the biggest Hong Kong registered fleets afloat. The wedding, in Amsterdam (where else?) had been followed by the London signing of merger documents. He even, for the first time, learned what the K stood for in the chairman's name. It was Kingsley. The Whippit-Snide Line was dead. Long live the Fu-King Line.

II

'You can go in now, sir,' the desk sergeant called, replacing the receiver. Across the room a sleepy Mr Pouch rose wearily from the bench. He'd been roused from his bed late last night and unwillingly escorted to his present location.

'Ah!' exclaimed the inspector, as if the last person he'd expected to appear was he.

'Come in, sir! Do come in...! Sign the visitor's book... That's right... Just there... Now please sit down.'

Mr Pouch did as bid, his perplexed expression scanning his surroundings. He noted the presence of a plain clothes officer and a police woman, pen poised over pad resting on her comely knee.

'Now then,' the inspector began, 'we sincerely apologize for inconveniencing you, which we regret has been necessary.' He cleared his throat as Mr Pouch sat in meek, puzzled silence. The inspector had already decided that during this interview he would use a little imagination, ignoring the usual well-worn phrases and constabulary clichés. His eyes lit up with sudden inspiration.

'Er... Mr Pouch... we... er... believe you may be able to help us in our enquiries regarding... er... well, I expect you are fully acquainted with the facts sir?'

'Facts?' repeated Mr Pouch, looking blank, and the WPC wrote down 'Facts?'

'Yes sir.'

'I'm not sure what you mean,' he said, and the eyes of the inspector narrowed.

'Are you *quite* sure?'

'Well... er... yes,' came the uncertain reply.

'Come now sir,' the inspector said, sounding as tired as Mr Pouch felt, 'she was your daughter.'

'She still is.'

'I mean... your daughter was the patient... right?'

'Yes.'

'And now she isn't?'

'Yes she is.'

The inquisitor scowled and addressed him curtly. 'You misunderstand. She is no longer a patient... she's absconded.'

'Has she really?' responded Mr Pouch in genuine surprise.

She really had – having been biding her time until the right opportunity presented itself. Tooting Bec Hospital was not unpleasant... for a few days, or weeks if necessary. It was warm, comfortable and she'd eaten far worse food. She would have preferred the privacy of her own place but if she had to remain there she would, for the time being. At least she didn't have to make her bed or do cooking. She could relax, take her medication dutifully, secure in the knowledge that her escape would be that much easier once staff had been lulled into a false sense of security.

Soon she would be wed to Captain Crawley Bix and travel the world free of charge, life transformed and dreams fulfilled. All she had to do in return was spread her legs occasionally, or bend over (who cared) while her lawful husband indulged himself. They even had something in common – *he* heard voices *too* sometimes, just like she did.

But oh! How she had agonised over letters to him. A certain discretion was demanded. Over-zealousness could prove her undoing – be disastrous in fact – and much of her anguish stemmed from uncertainties as to whether or not she had inadvertently been. Had she mentioned anything that could cast doubts on her respectability? He was, after all, a fine and noble ship's captain and wouldn't want to involve himself with any old scrubber. Then she would receive word from him and all would be well once more, until that is, she posted her reply and the agitation returned.

The inspector looked hard at Mr Pouch, asking, with practised skill, 'When did you see your daughter last, sir?'

'Oh... a few days back.'

'You visited her in hospital regularly, I believe?' Mr Pouch nodded assent and the WPC wrote 'nodded assent'.

'Now sir,' the inspector went on, 'would you please tell us why you sent for the ambulance in the first place?'

'It was her neighbour I wanted the ambulance for. Beatrice an' me had been to the pub. It was dark on the landing and she mistook him for someone else.'

'Even so...'

'What's that supposed to mean?'

'She attacks... nearly kills this man... and you visit her?' The inspector leaned on the desk, thoughtfully puckering his lips as if expecting a kiss. 'Hardly normal behaviour...'

'But... how else could I deliver the letters?'

'Ah *AH!*' The inspector jumped to his feet in elation. Now he was getting somewhere. A little carefully applied science and truth will out. He came around the desk and began to pace the floor behind the increasingly nervous Mr Pouch. 'There were *letters?*'

'Of course... I've just said...'

'What did these letters contain, Mr Pouch?'

'I don't know.'

'You didn't read them?'

'No.'

'Why? Weren't you just a wee bit curious?'

'No.'

'Because you knew what was in them all along?'

'No... If I'd read them... and I must admit it crossed my mind... she'd have known... she's too clever by half.' The inspector stooped down beside him and snapped.

'She may well be sir. She may well be... But I'd need more than the word of someone who writes letters and then gets curious as to their contents.'

'B...but...'

'It's only fair to warn you, sir... we know about the money.'

'Money?'

'The large withdrawal from Barclay's, Tooting Broadway... when you closed her account.'

'But...' The inspector leaned even closer and hissed.

'Where's that money now, Mr Pouch?'

'I... I... I... g...gave it to... Beatrice..'

'Oh!' The inspector feigned surprise. 'So you gave it to your daughter.'

'Well... yes.'

'We'd never have guessed... Why?'

'She... er... wanted me to.'

Returning to the comfort of his chair, the inspector nodded.

'I've no doubt of that. Vanishing tricks cost money y'know. There are people to pay, both inside and out.' He stared meaningfully at his startled victim. 'How much did *you* get?'

'Hey, wait a minute!' protested Mr Pouch. 'Just what are you implying? Are you suggesting that I...?'

The inspector smiled reassuringly. 'Now, now sir,' he said softly, 'I'm insinuating nothing of the kind. Who could possibly suspect a man of your integrity involving himself in such a serious escapade?' He paused once more, smiling at the WPC, hoping she was learning from his vast experience. She returned the smile thinking... 'What a fucking prat!'

'She was detained under the Mental Health Act, y'know... a possible danger to society.'

'I'm aware of that.'

'Then you will also be aware that such a patient cannot be discharged without written consent from the authorities. Social workers and medical staff both have to agree.'

'Yes,' sighed Mr Pouch, 'I know.'

'Did she visit your home tonight?'

'No.'

'Has she other relatives she might contact?'

'No.'

'What about friends?'

'None that I'm aware of.'

'What about the victim of this assault... He's back home now. Could she have gone somewhere with him?'

'Highly unlikely.'

'What makes you say that?'

'He's eloped... with another man.'

'Why not, indeed?' chuckled the inspector. 'It takes all kinds.' He steepled his fingers and put them thoughtfully to his lips. Watching Mr Pouch closely, he asked, 'Why did you write the letters and what did you say?'

The harassed father made to rise, only to discover a fourth party whose uniformed arm pushed him down.

'I'm waiting sir.'

'B...b...but I didn't! Honest!' He loosened his tie and undid the top button of his shirt. He was becoming uncomfortably warm. The inspector remained impassive as Mr Pouch continued. 'I mean... they were... bloody AIR MAIL letters! How... how could I...?'

'Air Mail letters?' The inspector's eyebrows arched, then fell flat in a frown.

'Yes.'

'From where?'

'Oh... various places... Africa, I think.'

The eyebrows shot up again. 'Africa?'

'Africa, yes.'

'Mmmmmmmm.'

Even more nervous, Mr Pouch watched as his interrogator's fingers annoyingly drummed the desk top, brow furrowed as he absorbed this new information. Surely this was *too* preposterous to even contemplate. Unquestionably a malicious fabrication. He would not give it credence. This man was treating the whole affair with outrageous frivolity! Did he really expect him to believe that an escape from Tooting Bec had been planned in Africa? He eyed Mr Pouch contemptuously.

'Since... er... having your only child carted away... have you suffered any... er... remorse?'

'Certainly not,' came the emphatic reply.

'Really? A man gets his only child committed and isn't at all sorry?'

'She's no child.'

'You're being flippant, Mr Pouch!'

'Anyway... she... er... needed treatment.'

'And you feel no sorrow... no pity?'

'Oh... well... sometimes.'

'So you *do* feel sorry?

'Sometimes... yeah,' admitted Mr Pouch, sweat beading

his brow. He was so tired and just wanted to go home.

'Ah! So you feel sorry, *sometimes*?' Mr Pouch nodded, sadly, and the questioning continued. 'Enough to… want to… make amends… expiate your guilt… re-establish yourself as the devoted…?'

'Oh, hell!' groaned Mr Pouch, dabbing his careworn face. 'I see what you're driving at inspector, but I wasn't *that* sorry, I'm afraid.'

'I see… so now you're *afraid*. Would you prefer to be sorry… have you a subconscious desire for punishment?'

'Oh Christ!'

'Let us return to this guilt complex.'

'I don't *have* a …'

'But you distinctly stated…' he turned to the WPC. 'Perkins, what did he distinctly say?'

'Well… sometimes,' she droned, looking up as if expecting a lump of sugar.

'You heard that…? You said…'

'WELL, I WAS BLOODY-WELL WRONG!'

'So now you're not sorry at all?' Mr Pouch nursed his dejected face in his hands and moaned.

'I'm not… happy… with her… situation, naturally.'

'You're not?'

'What father would be?'

'So you decided to do something constructive for her and…'

'TO HELL WITH THE LOT OF YOU!' Mr Pouch exploded in loud frustration. 'GOD! AFTER ALL I'VE BEEN THROUGH!' His shoulders heaved and the inspector was instant sympathy.

'It's been a strain, has it, sir?' The suspect nodded. 'Yes,' he went on softly, 'I imagine it has. You must have suffered terribly.' He came to his feet and stretched gratefully. 'Well, this has gone on long enough… you can go home now.'

'Wha…?'

'I said you can go home.'

'You… *mean* that?

'Of course, sir.'

'Ohhhhh!' Mr Pouch rose with a thankful sigh.

'You say she hasn't tried to contact you?'

'No. If she does I'll let you know.'

'That's highly commendable of you sir, highly commendable.'

'Thank you.'

'Constable Albright here will take you home.'

'Thank you very much.'

'He will also…' the inspector grinned, stifling a chuckle, '…bring you back when you've collected a few things.'

'What…?'

'Oh, you know the sort of stuff, toothpaste, shaving gear, change of underwear.'

Mr Pouch was lead dolefully off, quaking in his boots, as the plain clothes officer bounded forward retrieving the signed confession from the visitor's book… Truth will always out.

Dead Slow Ahead

Loaded to capacity, the S*usan Snide* cut low and cleanly, albeit somewhat sluggishly, through the South Atlantic swell. Listing slightly to starboard, her bow, freshly painted in Lourenco Marques and still unscarred, rose gently over the hump as if savouring the south easterly breeze. Then she'd creak softly over to port, dipping her nose in salute to the azure hill which moderately struck her bow, sending cooling spray over the sun-drenched fo'c's'le head below where dolphins played marine 'chicken', diving zigzaggedly ahead of her slicing hull. Silently fluttering flying fish broke surface, skimming free on translucent, delicate wing from the parting seas. Cape Town lay astern and the ocean lay stretched before her. Liverpool beckoning distantly – her seemingly effortless gait suggesting she knew of this, the sea supporting her as if she were as light as her captain's heart had previously been.

Hercules Duff strode onto the starboard wing of the bridge and indulged deeply of the bracing air. As if from nowhere an albatross appeared, gliding serenely no more than a few metres away, matching the vessel's speed and motion. The mate, instinctively swaying with each rise and fall, leaned contentedly on the rail smiling as he observed that which unhurriedly observed him, expressionless, possibly slightly mocking, he thought. Idly he wondered how such an ungainly, almost comical creature, could journey endlessly, seemingly coming from nowhere and going nowhere, through all weathers and, most perplexing of all, making little use of its great wingspan but utilizing air current to keep aloft.

Fearing reprisals in Cape Town, the Old Man had been all for pushing onto Dakar, Senegal, before seeking medical advice. He'd ignored the chief engineer's warning that there might be insufficient fuel, after his magnanimous dispensing of same by the bucket-full, for cooking and heating purposes, to any Lourenco Marquian who wanted some.

It was a warning Angus McKenzie could have bitten his tongue off for. Visions of lost consequences soon flooded and flickered across the screen of his vindictively inventive mind. Seeing himself resplendent as the chief prosecution witness when the solemn Lloyd's enquiry was convened to ascertain why a completely sea-worthy freighter should require salvaging on calm seas with her full complement of men still aboard.

'Aye... ah told 'im right enough, good sirs,' he heard himself avouching, 'an in nay uncertain manner. Ah didna' leave him in any doot as tae the liability, but...' here he would pause dramatically, '...he censured me for tryin' tae delude 'im, an' then doubted mah calculations' A touch of indignation would be merited here. '...Now, ah put it tae ye honourable gentlemen... *mah calculations wrong... after thirty years at sea, calculatin'?'* His eyes would gleam at the buzz from many a distinguished and titled throat. In his mind, chairs scraped on the marbled floor as noble heads nodded in agreement.

'Ex-Captain Bix...' the black-capped judge's portentous drone never failed to bring a pernicious twinkle to his dreamy eye and he grinned cruelly, '...you have been found guilty of an irreprievable act of gross negligence and irresponsibility. I have no alternative, after listening to the truthful, utterly reliable testimony of Chief Engineer Angus McKenzie, but to pronounce the supreme penalty. I hereby sentence you to be hanged by the neck until you are dead. The sentence to be carried out immediately. May the Lord *not* have mercy on your soul, in fact... *may you rot in hell!'*

Angus McKenzie would invariably hug himself as the final scene unfolded. The condemned man was led... nay, dragged, sobbing and squealing to the scaffold. The hooded executioner approaching with the noose for his trembling, cringing neck before pulling back his hood with slow, agonizing deliberation, to reveal the jubilant face of the newly-appointed shore superintendent engineer.

Glancing back at the attendant albatross, the mate re-entered the wheelhouse to join Nervous Purvis. He was pleased to have Cape Town behind him and especially the embarrassing circumstance surrounding their unscheduled visit. He could have warned the Old Man that those girls were probably afflicted with more than tribal markings. Still, it had only turned out to be gonorrhoea and not syphilis, which was something to be grateful for. The Old Man saw things differently.

In addition to injections of antibiotics administered by Chewsday, the only one aboard with the experience, he had been forced to cut back on his fluid intake. This was the lesser of the two by a mile as the passing of urine had become excruciating. Nonetheless, that party had really been something to write home about, although not in *too* much detail and certainly not to his Beatrice.

He'd been meticulous in its preparation. 'It'll only get in the way Stan,' he had remarked happily, back in L.M., scratching his chin in thought as he approvingly surveyed the increased space in the saloon. (The long dining table had been removed in readiness for the bride's farewell before her flight home to feather the love-nest.)

'Er… yes, I suppose it would, Crawley,' the steward had agreed disinterestedly, having decided to absent himself. 'You're probably right.'

'Mmmmm,' but the Old Man was far from done. Stabbing a finger towards a corner, he asked, 'Stanley, me boy! Would the bar look nice over there?'

'Er… yes. I…'

'Or… there?' he added, finger changing direction like that of a fastidious housewife re-arranging her living room. Bereft of any preference, Stanley Stone merely shrugged.

'She's your ship, Crawley,' he said.

'Now, now Stan,' he chided, 'don't be like that. It's not nice, and it's nice to be nice. She's *our* ship, not just mine… we all have a stake in her. Such is the modern attitude… makes for harmony on board.' He turned back to the corner. 'Yes,' he decided, 'that's where I want the bar. By the way... when can we expect the guest of honour?'

'About eight-thirty.'

'Good.' The Old Man was still on cloud nine and quietly chuckled at the frowning steward. 'Poor misguided wretch...,' he thought, '...friendless, lost and most likely as unfulfilled as he used to be, with only the sea for comfort. What a hopeless bloody life.'

'Shall I bring in the refreshments?'

'If you like, Stan. The cook has kindly done us a buffet, I believe.'

'He has, yes, Crawley. I'll summon assistance.' He turned to go and the Old Man called after him jovially, 'a bottle of rum each for the cook and the baker... with my compliments.' The steward left, dark scowl hidden from view.

As disdainfully as a royal butler required to wait tables in a Wimpy Bar, Stanley Stone had dutifully welcomed the visiting guests, escorting them to the saloon. Word had got out and the contingent of native girls had dramatically increased, each acting – it seemed to the steward – as if they, like the unsuspecting crew, had a stake in the vessel. He had barely returned to his cabin for some solitude when he heard the dinner gong being hammered like crazy, followed by the voice of the Old Man raucously bellowing, 'COME AND GET IT! COME AND GET IT! TONIGHT'S SPECIAL... HAIRY PIE!'

Within the hour an orgy had developed all over the cushion-strewn saloon deck and there, in the midst of it all, the be-robed, epicurean Old Man, sitting cross-legged, sipping beer and flanked on both sides by ebony nakedness. He lacked only a crown of laurel. There was even a lady teddy, brought aboard by one of the guests, with whom Tedward had had his wicked, lustful teddy-way behind a pile of beer cases, where they both now sat, glassy-eyed. Foreseeing what was to transpire, Hercules Duff and spouse had earlier departed graciously, following the initial announcement regarding the future of the Line.

* * *

'Common bloody trollops!' the Old Man had self-righteously declared, lips curling in disgust at the unseemly display on the quayside below. The Portuguese pilot had nodded agreement as the vessel moved away from her berth. The angry, unpaid girls were unwilling to be silenced and the Old Man's two were the most vociferous of them all. 'Sling 'em in jail,' he muttered, during their ranting at the departing ship, clearly and obscenely indicating what fate awaited him should he ever return. With a holier-than-thou sigh he said, 'Can't for the life of me see what my ratings see in the filthy whores... absolutely disgusting.'

True, he *had* promised much recompense, but one must be realistic. Just look at the perks they'd enjoyed – free food, drink, a hotel stay (of very short duration... but it was the principle) and what about the bonus of himself? Not a bloody engine room greaser, but a Captain... who had speedily become expert in the art of love-making. He shook his head in weary resignation. Some people were so ungrateful. Were they ever likely to encounter such again? And what about the party? Yes... they had been more than amply rewarded. Why the honour of being his sole guests for over a week should have been enough. In fact... they possibly owed *him* money! He had finally had to call upon the assistance of native dockers to carry them, kicking and screaming, ashore. The dockers had been only too pleased to repay his generosity by so doing.

'Poor Phoney,' said Mad McPhee leaning on a rail amidships, ''ope that bunch o' pricks don' get their 'ands on 'im.' Mahoney was adrift and his concerned shipmates, had, before the vessel sailed, intended a thorough search of the town, meeting up first in the Palace Bar to discuss tactics and getting no further.

'Wot bunch o' pricks?' asked Black Eye McKay.

'All *that* lot,' McPhee replied, motioning to the angry

gathering on the quayside.

'Y'mean the girls?'

'Yeah.'

''Ow can girls be pricks, you cunt?'

'He'll be okay,' assured the Snot Gobbler, 'don't go worryin' y' arse about 'im. 'E may have latched onto a couple o' ladies who love ladies. Betya 'e turns up in Custom House in a few months w' a tale as long as y' arm.'

'Course he will,' Chewsday said. 'That slimy phoney bastard can wriggle his way out of any problem. He's as phoney as Oskar Schindler.'

'Who's 'e?'

'Oh, some Nazi war-time Kraut I read about. Making a fortune from Jewish slave labour, he was. Then in nineteen forty four, he realized that Germany was going to lose the war and started protecting his slaves, saved many of their lives apparently. But he was really looking after number *one*, protecting his back. Which ever way the war ended he was going to survive with honours.'

They had been standing just outside the galley and the baker, overhearing them, came out. He'd been right through the Blitz in the East End, as a child, and doubted whether the scars would ever fade.

'Like those German generals,' he said, 'the ones who tried to kill Adolph. That wasn't until forty four either, when *they'd* realized the war was lost... Before then it was 'Heil Mein Fuckin' Fuhrer!'

'Anyway,' broke in the Treacle Bender, ''aven't y' heard the news t'day? Accordin' t' the radio, the Arabs and Israelis are at it again – knockin' all kinds o' shit outa each other an' the canal's being bombed.'

For the Old Man, this had been an unexpected bonus for which he'd dared not hope. He now had an official reason for returning via the Cape.

Once at sea again, the food had improved tremendously. This cheered the crew and they were in need of it for in Lourenco Marques a masquerading dry cleaner had come aboard and taken several of their best suits, never to be seen again. For the first time, the Old Man had actually begun visiting the galley and tasting the food before it was served up to his men. He was ensuring that his instructions regarding their welfare were being obeyed. Never had they seen him more salubrious. If this was another symptom of his madness, then long may it continue…

Freshly baked rolls and tab-nabs (cupcakes) were available every day and the main meals incomparable. Carnation milk now replaced the thick unsweetened stuff, and strawberry, raspberry and blackcurrant jam replaced greengage, greengage and greengage. There were cold cuts, cheese and biscuits available each evening and six cans of beer allowed, per man, per day. The *Susan Snide* was a happy ship, just as the Old Man had informed Beatrice it was.

'This won't fuckin' last,' scoffed Big Deal McNiel.

'Why not?' Robert enquired, uneasily.

''Cos I fuckin'-well say so, that's why.'

''Ow d'y' know?'

'It's not Whippet-Snide style.'

'They may 'ave changed.'

'Oh, they've changed all right. 'Aven't y' seen the new name plate above the mess door?'

They looked askance at one another before going to investigate, unaware that the chippie had spent time in his workshop the previous day fashioning a sign to replace the one which had read 'Crew's Mess', with one which read 'The Fu-King Restaurant'.

'Wassit mean?' asked Duncan, of no one in particular, as they stared, suspecting, but not fully aware of the valuelessness of any slim hope they had of remaining British Seamen.

The Old Man had been hopeful, once back at sea, that not only would he ensure his crew's contentment, but that the horrors of alcoholic withdrawal would not affect him. Grounds for such were based on the gradual decrease in consumption rather than sudden cessation. His normal reverence for the bottle had been, for the first time, replaced by release of years

– many such – of pent-up desire and he felt physically the better for it. Whisky was out. If in the morning he suffered hand tremors, then a couple of beers worked wonders. Oh how he wished for the witchdoctor to appear and turn the ship into a jet aircraft that he might reach Beatrice's side in hours.

'Each turn of the screw brings me nearer to you,' he would softly murmur. The thoughts of Hercules Duff were also miles away with the lady he cherished and thought of constantly.

'Every turn of the propeller brings me nearer my fella,' whispered Chewsday to himself, crossing the boat deck towards the Old Man's quarters with his injection, prescribed by a Cape Town doctor.

II

Stanley Stone was determined not to be crushed by the drastic change in circumstances. One door shuts... another one opens, and this time he had the support of a trusted and true friend, a compatriot of inestimable worth on whom he could totally rely. It was a relationship of enviable proportions based on mutual admiration and professional respect, tinged, he'd lately thought, with genuine affection.

The dormant seeds had lain untended for years, too engrossed had they been in their respective aspirations, but now he and the Old Man were inseparable and would remain so. His visions of Leadenhall Street status and subsequent glory irrevocably shattered, he clung to this belief like a mountaineer to his axe. Admittedly the Old Man was not a director, or anything quite so worshipful, but he *was* commodore master and that must count for something. But would he be commodore master of the new, vastly expanded Line or would the incumbent commodore master of the former Chung-Fu Line become commodore master of the whole shebang?

It was an extremely worrying aspect. Nor had they always seen eye to eye but this happened in the most fruitful of unions... didn't it? Of *course* it did! Even Gilbert and Sullivan hated each other's guts from time to time and look what they produced as a team! Mind you... there was no evidence that one had jealously tried to poison the other... the memory filled him with shame.

'Ah!' exclaimed the Old Man heartily, after sailing, stepping sprightly over the storm-step into the galley, sniffing the air appreciatively, followed by the chief steward. 'Something smells nice.'

'Er... thanks... er... sir,' stammered the cook, who had never received a compliment in his life and blushed with embarrassment under the scowl of Mr Stone.

This had been the first of several visits paid each morning at 1145 hrs, which promptly and inexplicably ended shortly before the unscheduled arrival at Cape Town. It was assumed by *almost* everyone on board that the Old Man had simply lost interest. But for this first visit, the cook and baker had been forewarned and everything was ready for the Old Man to sample – small portions of pea and ham soup, braised steak, creamed potatoes, carrots and sprouts, followed by fruit and ice cream.

'Mmmmmm,' he murmured, sipping tentatively at the soup. 'This is very good, cook. Very good indeed.'

'Thank y', sir,' he replied, smiling broadly, chest inflated.

'You know,' the Old Man said, investigatively chewing on the steak and addressing Stanley Stone, 'if this standard is maintained all the way home, the lads should be well content.'

'Of course,' he replied, smiling thinly as he grimly dwelt on the cost.

'And that's what we want... isn't it Stanley?'

'Oh, most assuredly, Crawley.'

The mood of his men was not the only factor in all this. He had no wish for Beatrice to overhear complaints regarding their nourishment. If she got the impression that he lacked concern for those under his command...then what treatment could *she* expect?

'Ah well,' he said, beaming and making for the door, 'keep up the good work you two.'

'We'll do our best, sir,' the cook and baker replied in unison.

To be fair to them, the quality, variety and quantity of provisions allowed by Stanley Stone had done naught to help them reach, let alone pass, a mediocre standard, so they hadn't tried overmuch. But improved stores and the prospect of daily inspection by the Old Man gave them no alternative but to pull their fingers out.

The possible enforced removal from ship to shore gave the chief steward the heeby-jeebies. What on earth would he do? He must focus his mind. He had no knowledge of the rigors of modern shore society and just wouldn't fit it. He was only approaching fifty, same as the Old Man, and although not short of money – his nest egg being a disgustingly healthy shade of green – he could not afford to retire. He rightly suspected that the company would now be sailing under the Hong Kong flag and that Asians would be replacing all British seamen, as they already had on many British fleets. This meant different food, different cooks, different stewards. It was possible he may be able to hang onto his post as *chief* steward initially, but what then?

When barely a child he had realized that everyone, even the most honest, moral and righteous individual, eventually dies so he had excluded himself from those categories because they were, to a man or woman, not rich. 'Thy will be done on earth as it is in heaven' surely meant that the wealthy would thus awaken on the other side while the poor were doomed to an eternity of deprivation on an overcrowded slum cloud, without the means to soar to more select heights. No, 'Thy will be done…' The elite were even up there and he'd join them even if it killed him.

But for now he was safe with the admirable, born-again Crawley. True, expenditure had risen astronomically, severely restricting his scope, but he could see no one else between him and the shoreside scrap heap. He needed him, his help, his influence, his friendship. Life has it ups and downs. The company's merger had been a down, next would come an up…

But he was wrong. It was another down.

'Wod I *tell* yer?' sang Big Deal McMiel, pointing smugly to his leathery eggs and soggy chips. 'Ah *told* yer so! Ah said it wouldn't last!'

'Okay! Okay!' snapped Downtown Daley. 'Don't friggin' rub it in. Y' said it wouldn' last!'

''Cos ah knew it wouldn't…that's why.' His smirk suggested that his pleasure at being right outweighed the disadvantages. 'First the beer was stopped and now *this.*'

'Wot d'y' suggest we do about it?' Black Eye McKay wanted to know.

'Ah'm not suggestin' anything. I just said it wouldn't fuckin' last an' it didn't.'

The Treacle Bender put forward the idea of a hunger strike.

'Y' can't do that,' One Way Rodgers said, who'd surprisingly not jumped ship.

'Why not?' Suitcase Larson asked.

'Becos…' he patiently explained, 'if y' don't eat, y' don't shite, an' if y' don't shite… y' die.'

'What I can't understan',' mused Duncan, unconcerned about the deteriorating food but not about the beer ration, 'is wot's *'appened* to it? I saw it being loaded myself in L.M.'

'An' if y' look closely,' broke in the Treacle Bender, still smarting over Froggy the Moggy's failure to return to the ship, 'you'll most likely see it going ashore agin in Dakar.'

'Y'mean flogged?'

'Wot else?'

'By the chief steward?'

'Who else?' They used to call him Robin Hood, now they call him robbin' bastard.

'Well, let's ask Chewsday or the Gobbler t' keep an eye on 'im. They live an' work amidships, 'e's their boss.'

'I doubt if even they know wot's goin' on.'

'Then we'll report it t' the Old Man.'

''E don't come aroun' anymore, does 'e?'

'Mmmmmmm… I wonder why.'

The Cape of Good Hope had not been far ahead when the Old Man's indisposition began. Stanley Stone was distressed to find him recumbent on his daybed, apparently unwell.

'Crawley, my dear fellow,' he asked, concerned, 'whatever is the matter?'

'Oh... nothing,' the Old Man replied sourly, his attempt at a smile becoming a grimace as he was further asked, with fraternal solicitude, 'Is there anything I can do?'

'No, no. Nothing at all.'

But he remained unconvinced. Something was definitely amiss.

'A drink, perhaps... or something? Is there anything special you'd like for lunch?'

'No.' this time he sounded a little irritated. 'There is nothing you can do.' He got up and stiffly approached the door, intending to close it on the persistent steward whose eyes pleaded for permission to help the one man alive who could salvage his career.

But the Old Man required his symptoms to be known only to his trusted chief mate at this point. Even so, he paused at the door and voiced the question, which had occupied his mind since the onset of his discomfiture.

'Er... by the way, Stan... er...' he was trying to sound matter-of-factly, '...has anyone else... I mean... is any of the ship's company... er... sick?'

The steward scratched his head. 'Sick?'

'Yes... you know... the usual... gons?'

'Oh, that,' he chuckled. 'No Crawley... I'm surprised... naturally... after that party... But I'm happy to say they've all escaped it.'

The Old Man's enforced casualness was being slowly usurped by pressure building like gas in a blocked main and he glared at the innocently grinning steward as indeed did Tedward, quite menacingly.

'None at all?' he whined, and the steward, mistaking his distress for comic disbelief, threw back his head in guffaws of jollity.

'None at all!' he happily repeated, heaving with merriment at his buddy's wrongly perceived jocularity. And then… he said the one thing, which struck the match. 'Not even the *engineers.'*

That was it. Having the blasted pox was bad enough but being the only one on the blasted ship…! Ruptured main and match coincided and Stanley Stone was to bear the scars for life. From then on, he knew his seafaring days were numbered. Some Indonesian who would work for a fraction of the pay and not be able to understand a word of English would almost certainly replace him. Plan 'B' was the ownership of a country pub and the more he could salt away between now and Liverpool, the better.

If the Old Man had felt unwell before, he now felt worse and oh, so terribly ashamed. Alone in his quarters he hurled noisy vilifications on everyone, reserving the choicest for the two girls who had actually wanted *PAYING!* If not for fear of aggravating his condition, he would have drowned his woes in scotch.

Another sorrow was Beatrice. Dear, sweet Beatrice, who could charm the birds from the trees. In every letter she would enquire and hope for his continuing good health… Oh, for shame! How often had he reviled a rating for not taking the simplest of precautions…? And now…

'Oh, the filthy cows!'

Putting into Cape Town to seek medical attention for the Old Man had been Hercules Duff's idea. 'Just to be on the safe side, sir,' he'd said, and for once the Old Man didn't argue, knowing full well that it could have been much worse.

Homeward-bound at last, the *Susan Snide* was undergoing a comprehensive sprucing up for neither the Old Man, nor Hercules, wanted to arrive, watched by their respective ladies, in a vessel looking as though she'd been dredged from the seabed. From the monkey island above the wheelhouse, downwards, her superstructure was being transformed from its usual dirty cream to a brilliant white, painful to the eyes in the bright sun. Derricks, winches and samson posts, masts and mast houses, were being thoroughly washed with suji powder in preparation for the long overdue coat of battleship grey. The bosun and his lads were in their element.

The engine-room too was not being ignored. Bulkheads were being white-coated and all auxiliary machinery in green. Even the boilers were receiving a covering of silverene. Not a rating on board had any complaint about the non-stop work because the overtime was being clocked-up to complete the job. The vessel echoed with committed activity and the passage promised to be both peaceful and profitable. Then tragedy struck.

'What the...?' gasped the Old Man breathlessly, having been urgently summoned by the mate to Chewsday's cabin. Oddball McCall lay unconscious on the bunk, head and shoulders propped up with pillows. 'What's wrong?'

'It's McCall, sir,' he was informed. 'He's been seriously injured.'

'He's got a nasty head wound, Captain,' added Chewsday, holding a dressing firmly in place.

'Shouldn't he be lying flat?'

'Not with a head injury sir.' The Old Man nodded. Of course he should have remembered that, and had life not been such a bastard to him recently, he would have done.

'I've stopped the bleeding, but...' went on Chewsday, head shaking sadly, 'he's in need of medical treatment fast.'

'He's getting it, isn't he? Weren't you in the Medical Corps?'

'He means professional treatment, sir.' Stanley Stone, who was also present, explained. He didn't call him Crawley anymore.

'I'm not a magician, steward,' he said. He didn't call him Stanley anymore either.

'What happened?' he snapped accusingly, at the mate.

'He fell from a samson post.'

'Did anyone see it?'

'Several men.'

'Ah... but were there any *officers* present?'

'What's that got to do with it?'

'Every-bloody-thing! He could be throwing a wobbler.'

'But he's...' Chewsday broke in, to be silenced.

'A *phoney!*' the Old Man cried. '*Steward! Give this man a codeine tablet. I want him back at work!*' He then stormed out.

Hercules Duff wrung his hands. He had been mistaken in assuming that the dose of clap was heaven sent to cure the Old Man of his drink addiction. I mean... why would God bother? He wasn't worth it. He was a fool, drunk or sober... No, that was far too lenient. He was *mad!* Poxed-up or pissed up, it made no difference. Then the Old Man was back, blustering and protesting as the big, burly frame of Hard Nut Neilson propelled him forwards.

To his horror, Neilson had witnessed the accident and helped carry McCall to the bunk where Chewsday began working on him at once. He had discretely retired when the Old Man arrived, to sit and grieve on deck.

'Oh Christ!' he moaned, it had been a bad fall. He'd seen him land. 'Run me down in a lifeboat anytime... Just please...!' His chin dropped despairingly to his hairy chest. '...Please don't let 'im die... 'e never did no one no 'arm.' It was then he'd overhead the Old Man's angry protestations and without considering the consequences, ran back inside.

'*'E's not a phoney an' 'e's not throwin' a wobbler,*' he yelled at the stunned captain. '*Just look at 'im! Look at him!*' He'd grabbed the Old Man by the back of the head, forcing him to look.

The Old Man WAS looking, blankly. For the past few days he hadn't been eating, sleeping or thinking clearly, but worrying constantly about his condition and about Beatrice. And now he was being manhandled by a *rating*, who he could have clapped in *irons*... But at the back of his mind somewhere was the realization that *he* was in the wrong.

'ARE YOU LISTENING T' ME, CAPTAIN?' Hard Nut Neilson was shaking him, none too gently, having thrown all caution to the winds. He would never sail again and could even be thrown in jail for assaulting the master at sea, but Oddball's life was all he cared about just then.

'Er… yes… YES,' the Old Man heard himself say through the haze of shock. 'Er... who are you?'

'FUCKIN' NEILSON! AN' THAT'S MY MATE, DYIN' OVER THERE!'

The Old Man was gazing at the unconscious McCall, when suddenly something snapped within him. 'MR DUFF!' he barked, 'tell the sparks to get onto Dakar – as soon as we are within range. I want a helicopter flown out with a doctor!'

Almost ready to fall asleep on his feet, the Old Man wearily turned to go, then stopped. 'Neilson,' he said tiredly, 'get the bosun up to my quarters. I want a lifeboat made ready for launching… there maybe a vessel in the area with medical staff on board… Oh and steward…'

'Sir?' said Stanley Stone.

'Get a stretcher checked over.' He got to the door and turned once more. 'Second steward?'

'Sir?'

'Look after the lad as best y'can.'

With that he staggered, dog tired, to his cabin where, after phoning the bridge to order maximum revolutions, he collapsed onto his bed where he slept the sleep of the dead. For how long he slept he had no idea but was awoken to learn that a French military helicopter was on its way.

Stop

The second engineer was thrilled with the engine's performance, but not with the chief's, who had not rewarded him with the commendation he felt entitled to. That the homeward passage had been as smooth and dependable as a Rolls Royce was, he assumed, solely attributable to the work he'd directed while the chief was in hospital. When the mail came aboard in Dakar he was also delighted to learn that none was addressed to him for his estranged wife would ignore his whereabouts unless learning that he was homeward bound with money. Obviously she was still unaware of this, so he may decide not to pay her a visit.

'Why don't you show your feminine side? You uncouth, slob bastard.' Had been her regular carp.

He, convinced that any woman who wanted that didn't want a man at all, would invariable respond with, 'Ya' mean like you show y' masculine one? You moustachioed fuckin' ol' rag.' A marriage made in heaven it was not.

Angus McKenzie experienced similar emotions for if any reputation-enhancing plaudits were in the offing for a trouble-free homecoming then he, as commodore chief, would receive every last one. But more importantly, in the short term, her recent reliability had allowed him to ignore the engine room completely.

Since McCall's accident, the Old Man had become reclusive, not even visiting the bridge to avoid coming face to face with Neilson on the wheel. Even Tedward had fell glumly silent of late. Everything had been left to Hercules Duff, including the despatch of the injured seaman by helicopter.

Logging ratings for misdemeanours was part and parcel of his job but nothing as serious as this had ever happened to him and he wasn't quite sure how to handle it. On the one hand, Neilson's behaviour had been unforgivable, almost *mutinous*, but on the other, he was excruciatingly aware that his own had been downright inhumane, a disgrace to his rank. Neilson himself, knocking on the Old Man's door just after arrival in Dakar, profusely apologizing and begging for permission to visit McCall in the French Military Hospital, provided a way out of the dilemma. A moment earlier and he would have passed the doctor, leaving.

The Old Man was in especially good heart. He had been medically informed that his condition was all but eliminated. To Neilson's amazement he was cordially invited in and told to take a seat. The Old Man was bursting with pride on another matter too. Whilst in Cape Town, he'd had several drums of fuel oil delivered in case the warnings he'd received about running short proved correct. But she'd made it to her bunkering port without them being needed which clearly proved Angus McKenzie's calculations wrong.

'But he's still in a coma,' he explained to Neilson.

'I can at least *see* 'im.'

'But he won't be able to see *you*.'

'What difference does *that* make?'

'What *is* it with you and McCall anyway... are you *that* close?'

'Yes we are sir,' he explained. 'We went to school together an' went to sea together, an' for the last three years we've... ah mean... we'd sailed together several times before that, but since then it's always been together.'

The Old Man had both McCall and Neilson's discharge books on the desk before him – McCall's was being sent to the hospital – and was scrutinizing them.

'I see you're both from the Norfolk area.'

'More than that, sir. Three years ago we married twin sisters and live not far apart.'

'Oh!' the Old Man sounded surprised. 'So you are each the other's brother-in-law?'

'Yeah, an' when we got married I 'ad to make a pact with

'is missus and 'e 'ad to make a pact wi' mine, otherwise… no more sailin'.'

'Pact?'

'Yeah… that we took care o' each other, an' in particular, that we kept each other away from loose birds and whores. If I ever slipped up I know 'e'd report back t' the wife, an' ah'd do the same t' him. It's worked well for the past three years.'

'Look Neilson,' nodded the Old Man, 'I can't allow any shore leave in a bunkering port. We'll be off again in a few hours. Everything is being done for him, believe me. If I hear any further word on his condition, you'll be the first to know.'

The Old Man sounded almost compassionate but he was already short of a fireman – Mahoney, and McCall. He simply could not risk losing another able seaman. Soon there will be no one left!

'I suggest that you write a letter and slip it into his gear. I'm detailing you, along with the second mate, to pack his bags for the hospital.'

Neilson didn't reply but stared sullenly before him thinking that he may as well jump ship anyway and go to Oddball. After all, following his physical display of anger with the Old Man, he probably had nothing to lose.

'And if you're thinking of jumping ship because you have nothing to lose… forget it. I'm giving you a very good discharge, in fact… it might be V.G.s all round.'

'But…' he said, frowning with disbelief at the Old Man who held up his hand.

'I've considered your action and taken into account your close friendship and family connections and believe that you had no wish to defy me other than to assist McCall. Therefore I propose to drop the matter. You can go now.'

Neilson left in silence, not daring to speak in case he'd misheard everything the Old Man had said.

Then Stanley Stone arrived with three letters from Beatrice, sending him into raptures of delight as each reiterated her avowed intention to be in Liverpool for his entrance, which he'd decided was going to be the most spectacular the city had ever seen – returning Beatles included.

'Royal Yacht?' he murmured dreamily, 'eat your heart out.' The welcome news from the doctor, the welcome news from Beatrice, coupled with his handling of the dicey situation a` la Neilson, called for some celebratory scotch which had gone straight from the cabinet and straight to his head. He took to his daybed singing softly...

'When he fancies he is past love,
It is then he meets his last love,
And he loves her like he's never loved before.'

He was in an unfamiliar room. Everything was bathed in a peculiar, misty, unearthly glow. The mist clung to his bare ankles but he felt no cold. There was an imposing bed, an ornate four-poster it was, and he found himself floating towards it. A door opened which he'd not noticed being there, and an apparition entered with long flowing hair, in a garment of gossamer, both of which fluttered in a breeze he himself could not feel. Silently she drew closer, her features clarifying until... Lo and behold... Ms Beatrice Pouch from Burnham-on-Crouch!'

Ecstatically he bounded forward, arms spread wide in which to enfold her but a raised hand bade him stay. She halted, the garment wafting to her feet. Like Venus she stood and he, transfixed, lips parted with desire as trembling hands moved to undress, only to learn that he was already naked. Her gaze descended longingly; pausing on his manliness, tongue sliding across her glistening upper lip.

Then her jaw dropped in horror, sultry eyes now filled with repugnance and loathing as she hurriedly backed towards the door, her delicate palms keeping him at bay. Then she was gone – vanished forever into infinity. Wailing in anguish, he looked down at that which had caused such distress and the wailing from his damp face became a despairing howl. His organ was emitting a bubble. Not an ordinary bubble but a venereal bubble and he awoke lathered in sweat, tossing fitfully and crying, *'Come back! Come back, dearest heart! I'm cured! CURED!'*

* * *

Back at sea again, Stanley Stone had also awoken, thankful for
his deliverance from such a harrowing nightmare in which, in
his eagerness to make a final killing before the end of his final
voyage, he'd sold every last bottle of scotch on board, along
with almost everything else, only to learn that the Old Man
was off the wagon.

Now he *too* was lathered in sweat and it was no dream.

He sat bolt upright, ears cocked. Was that whispering he
heard in the alleyway beyond his door? Now there were
definite *voices* and... yes... MY GOD! Someone was trying
the LOCK! Had he only dreamt that the dream was over? Was
he still asleep? He pinched himself and it hurt, but would not a
dream pinch also hurt?

'We know you're in there, chief.'

Good grief! It was the engine-room storekeeper. What in
the same of...? 'Go away!' he cried, 'I'm asleep.'

'Y' will be when we've finished w' ya! The chippie's on
'is way. He'll 'ave this door off in no time.'

'What the hell...?'

This time the voice had been that of the bosun, who hadn't
finished.

'The Old Man's given us permission t' punish ya 'owever
we please... An' 'ave *we* got a *way.*'

The alleyway then resounded with laughter and cheers as
hammer blows rained on the door.

'GO AWAY! LEAVE ME ALONE!' he shrieked, now fully
aware of consciousness.

'Steward! Open this door!' Now it was the Old Man.
*'NOW. If you don't it will be broken. After that it will be your
head!'*

'Ohhhhhhhhhhhhhhhh!' came the submissive cry from
Stanley Stone. He got up and dressed, hoping his little gold
braid would deter physical harm from the ratings. On opening
the door, he immediately fell back in terror, crumbling lifeless

as the petty officers bounded in, the Old Man bringing up the rear. He was caught before a potentially heavy fall and propped up, shaking like a pneumatic drill.

'Now,' the Old Man began, 'if you're quite ready.'

'R...r...ready... s...sir?'

'That's what I said.'

'F...f...for... w...what?'

'To pay the penalty for your greed.'

'Can we rephrase that sir...' asked the chippie thro' a self-satisfied grin, '...to be cleansed?' For some reason unknown to the steward, this was received with an outburst of tittering.

'B...b...but... w...why sir?' he stammered.

'DO MY EARS DECIEVE ME?' the Old Man screamed. He was livid. 'You have the audacity to ask THAT?' Making a rough grab, he shook him by the shoulders and raised an involuntary fist before the bosun broke in, semi-chidingly.

'Now, now sir... you *promised*.'

Closing his eyes and counting to ten, by which time he'd regained a degree of composure, the Old Man sighed. 'You're right, bosun. Almost forgot meself.' He glared at the wobbling steward and roared, '*WELL... Come on... We haven't got all bloody day!*'

'Where... t...t...t...to...?'

'On deck. We're all waiting for you.' He turned to the E.R.S. 'Stores... are all the weapons prepared?'

'Yeah, Cap'n,' he replied, eyes shone as he nodded in joyful anticipation. 'They're in the Fu-King Restaurant.'

'*The WHAT?*'

'Blame me for that sir,' offered the chippie. 'I changed the name o' the Crew's Mess. The weapons are in the 'otpress which doesn't work.'

The Old Man's face spread in a smile of appreciation. 'The Fu-King Restaurant,' he mused. 'I *like* it, chippie. I *like* it. Very astute.'

'I mean... with the company flaggin' out an'...'

'I know chippie, I'm not happy about it but my hands are tied. British seamen have been good enough for centuries, now they are all being slung on the beach like discarded French Letters, replaced by foreigners who'll work for next to nothing. But that's not all. It's a clever tax dodge. Foreign registration means no British taxes, the seamen won't have a union to protect their interests and the owners can ignore British maritime rules and regulations, including those on safety. They'll save a fortune and that's what it's all about. Patriotism is meaningless to these people where money's concerned. But the big joke is… some of these owners are sitting in the House of Lords, drawing expenses paid for by the same taxpayers they're ripping off. I am sure it is obvious that the British ship owner is wiping his greedy, fat, corporate arse on the Red Ensign, before it vanishes from the sea entirely. Our once proud island nation is becoming an abomination where flags of convenience are very convenient indeed for the British ship owner and the purpose of tax avoidance. They much prefer the word avoidance to dodging but we all know that it amounts to the same thing.'

He had been talking to them, not as their Captain, but as their friend and all present (apart from Stanley Stone) nodded in solemn acquiescence. Then the Old Man snapped into action again, barking at the steward.

'I said we don't have ALL DAY! GET MOVING!'

The hairs on the steward's neck bristled in fear as, squealing like a piglet, he dived for his bed where he lay, cringing and whimpering, as he endeavoured to vanish into the mattress. Saliva ran freely from the corner of his mouth.

'I…I…I… can… ex…explain… sir…'

'Oh?' the Old Man asked, in mock surprise. 'Can you?'

'Y…y…ye…'

'Well you're not getting the flaming chance. The lads came to me with a complaint, after which I searched the provisions and bonded stores. They've been RANSACKED, you bastard! PLUNDERED! There's almost bugger-all left, and y'know why… because you've SOLD IT… THAT'S why! You selfish, greedy snivelling bastard! How long has *this* been going on… *YEARS,* I shouldn't wonder! Right under my trusting *nose! That's* what rankles me! You've even cleared out the Scotch.'

'This doesn't say much for *my* capabilities, does it, you bastard!'

'B...b...but...'

'No more buts. GET UP! We're WAITING!'

'H...h... who?'

'All *hands, that's* who.'

'Eeeeeeeeeeee! Eeeeeeeeeeeeeeeeee! No...! No...! No...! N...n...not the... cr...crew...! Sir...!'

'And why not? They're on starvation rations *and* you've flogged the beer!' Putting his loathing face up against the steward's he hissed, 'Not to mention the blasted scotch.'

'EEEEEEEE! I'm dr...dr...dream...ing. Wake me... up... somebody... *PLEASE!*

'Oh... you'll wake up all right... Bosun?'

'Sir?'

'Enough of this frigging nonsense... take him out.'

'With pleasure sir,' came the unified response as three pairs of arms, itching with revenge, grabbed him.

He was frog-marched outside, blinking with fright, too numb to further struggle or protest. The engine had been stopped especially and the bridge was deserted. His lap of dishonour between lines of jeering men, was interspersed with painful prods from an array of knives, boathooks and marlin spikes. His mouth would periodically open to give vent to his agony but vocal cords were paralysed. Wide-eyed he stumbled on as they pushed and jostled enthusiastically for his blood. It was a scorching day yet the sweat on his face was like the condensation in the pantry fridge. Inwardly he screamed for deliverance from this nightmare which had mistaken the time of day. Loudly they bayed around him like pursuing hounds. Oh for sweet reality, to find sanctuary in unconsciousness and emerge, restless, crying... but safe upon his bunk.

His eyes closed as the parade stopped and his captors released their blood-restricting grip. Forced to move on, he again prayed for oblivion. He looked down to see why the deck suddenly felt so odd beneath him and immediately stopped praying for oblivion for he stood precariously on a plank, stretching out over the side as unsteady as a diving board. Instinctively he stepped back but was obliged to continue forward as pointed steel, in perforating jabs, assailed him painfully. It was all he could do to maintain his balance as the plank sprang beneath his weight. The green hungry-looking sea was most uninviting. The further he was forced to tread, the less safe he felt and the delighted clamour increased in volume.

'*Picked up the 'Judith' sir!*' shouted the approaching sparks above the din. The Old Man was standing on the hatch cover to savour it all the better and seemed to be enjoying himself immensely.

He felt as though he had regained his standing with the men – *improved* on it even, to be held in higher esteem by ratings than ever before in his life. And why shouldn't he let them enjoy themselves? As far as it concerned *them*, the Merchant Navy was as good as dead in the water – their jobs were vanishing hand over fist so they could take this business as far as they wanted. When they cheered, he cheered. When they hurled abuse, so did he. He was unashamedly revelling and considered the lads were handling matters extremely well as he frequently dabbed blissful tears flooding his pleasure-filled eyes.

The sparks climbed up to stand beside him. '*Picked up the 'Judith',*' he repeated. '*Captain Anderson sends his regards!*'

'Oh, yes?' The Old Man was too engrossed to take much notice. 'Jolly nice of him.'

'*She's bound for Liverpool, sir.*'

Tearing his enthralled gaze reluctantly from the spectacle, he turned to face him. '*I'm sorry sparks,*' he said, '*I didn't quite catch...*'

'*She's headed for Liverpool, sir.*'

Nodding, the Old Man returned his grinning face to the entertainment. '*What's her position?*'

'*Just fifty miles astern, sir.*'

The cheering was reaching a crescendo when the Old Man's grin froze, then vanished completely.

'Fifty miles astern?'

'About that sir, yes.'

'Where the hell's she been?'

'Recife. Bunkered homeward bound in Los Palmas.'

The Old Man's attention was once more on the chief steward but this time he was scowling. Stanley Stone tottered on the brink as the plank bobbed and quivered. His tormenters could not reach him now, being unwilling to venture out after him. Angus McKenzie emerged from the galley with some cleavers as the full implications of the news struck the Old Man.

'QUIET!' he yelled. 'QUIET EVERYONE! THAT'S ENOUGH!'

'Aw, but sir,' moaned the bosun in disappointment, 'you bleedin' *promised!'*

'I know bosun, but...'

'Well, can we let go the plank?'

The Old Man smiled. 'Be my guest,' he said, and the gibbering steward careered into the sea, the plank close behind.

'Right!' the Old Man cried, jumping athletically from the hatch, *'fun's over! Everyone back to their duties!'* He then ran to Angus McKenzie who was happily hurling cleavers at the floating victim who was using the plank for protection.

'Angus!' he exclaimed, urgently grabbing his shoulders and spinning him round.

'The *Judith* is fifty miles astern. We must bury the hatchet Angus, our reputations are at stake.'

'Wha... the...?' muttered the annoyed and puzzled engineer, and the Old Man repeated his tale, eyes wide with concern, adding 'She is making damned good progress but she must not reach Liverpool before *we* do.' He took out a handkerchief and began mopping his brow. 'So you see, we must...'

But he was talking to himself. Angus McKenzie was already clambering down into the engine-room, barking orders.

With every furnace flashed up and steam pressure at maximum, he opened up the engine without waiting for the telegraph to ring.

This was *bloody appalling!* It could send his hopes of promotion nose-diving into shit creek. If it meant bringing down his mattress to sleep by the engine, so help him, he'd do it. He must not be humiliated by the *Judith*. If the flagship, with himself in charge of propulsion, was overtaken by that clapped-out barge, he'd never live it down. Why... the *Judith's* chief engineer might even be given the post of... No... it was unthinkable. *Bloody unthinkable!*

Fretting interminably, the Old Man paced the bridge, blasting his misfortune. To have that reptile Anderson threatening his grand arrival was catastrophic and he warned all concerned of the fate awaiting them if the vessel veered even fractionally off course. There would be pinpoint navigation from now on. The days dragged and the nights were sleepless – then came the impudent message from the *Judith* claiming still to be gaining on the *Susan* despite stopping to rescue a steward, clinging to a plank, and begging to be woken up. The insolent 'Do you require his return when we pass you?' sent both the Old Man and the chief engineer howling and cursing to every corner of the ship.

This was no idle boast. A smoking blotch astern grew ever closer. The *Susan*, although responding well, was being pushed to her very limits, but Angus McKenzie, eyes swollen from sleeplessness, was far from satisfied. Four days later they were half a mile apart. Thus they reached Biscay and the desperate engineer was torturing his brain to devise a way of stopping this upstart in her watery tracks.

II

Beatrice... Beatrice... Beatrice, occupied the Old Man's mind like drug withdrawal as inch by cheeky inch, yard by insolent yard, the threatening form of the *Judith* closed on her younger sister. Oh what ridicule he would suffer, and rightly so, when he manoeuvred into port behind her. Anderson's uncouth mob would be bad enough... but Beatrice...! *Fifty bloody miles...* *Fifty bloody miles* ahead and then shown a clean pair of heels by a hulk due for the breakers. He would warrant all the mockery there was.

'Anderson, you bastard!' he snarled, gazing astern from the wing of the bridge towards the ominously looming indignity. It was then he decided not to appear on the bridge wing again in full view of, he had no doubt, the jubilant binoculars of his pursuers. No, in future he would satisfy curiosity by playing 'peek-a-boo'. If Anderson was after the commodore master's post he was going the right way about it. Two days more and the difference was down even further.

Each sly glance only increased the Old Man's anxiety, sending him into the frustrated rages he thought he'd banished. But what was he to do? How was he to react when on several occasions he witnessed, through his own trembling binoculars, officers on the *Judith* skipping and dancing confidently across her bridge, with Captain Anderson playing the role of Pied Piper?

'Oh, the *bastards*,' he would growl, eyes closing in painful resignation.

Angus McKenzie was resolute. 'Sling more men over the wall,' had been one eager suggestion, 'so that prick has t' stop an' pick 'em up!'

'I only wish I could Angus,' the Old Man replied, shaking his head sadly, 'but the sod would probably leave them to die, that's if he noticed them at *all*. His glasses are trained on *us!*'

'Mmmmmm.'

'And besides... who's going to finish all the painting? We can't arrive second *and* unfinished!'

'Over my dead body!' snapped the engineer.

Angus McKenzie had been pacing the engine-room deck plates, his aching brain feverishly working to unravel, to find a solution or a suitable deterrent, but his eyes were ever vigilant for potential mechanical calamities. He trusted no one, and the most marginal fluctuation in steam pressure would send him charging into the stokehold, shouting to the fireman, *'she's up and doon like a whore's drawers! Keep it up! Keep it up!'*

Incessant pleas from the distraught Old Man wore out his fragile patience and he left the receiver off the hook. It was during this resultant respite he found his intellectually devious summit and almost collapsed with relief.

'G'mornin' sparks!' he called, as they entered the radio room together. Angus was even smiling, dreamily, as he asked for Captain Anderson. Soon, the expected jocularity came over the air.

'Hello there *Susan Snide*! Anderson here. Anything I can do for you? Over.' He did nothing to disguise his unmistakable glee and the Old Man winced. Angus McKenzie grabbed the receiver.

'Remember me, Anderson?' he growled, 'Angus McKen...?'

'I do indeed Angus. How could anyone fail to? To what do I owe this honour? Having trouble with that sewing machine you call an engine?'

'WHY YOU...!' He was about to toss the handset away and jump on it when the Old Man snatched if from him.

'Anderson,' he said gravely, 'this is the commodore...'

'My *MY*!' came the unimpressed reply. 'I really *am* honoured. Hello there, Bix...! I wondered when you'd get around to call me. What seems to be...?'

'Just listen...'

'What is it you require... a *tow?* Over.'

Gnashing dentures, the Old Man spat each word. 'Listen Anderson... we have a cargo of high explosives. War has erupted between India and Pakistan in Middlesbrough. It is imperative that we be given priority...!'

'Nice try, Bix old chap. I don't believe a word. You're just windy because you know you're beaten.'

'It's the TRUTH, I tell you!'

'What do you *take* me for? Nobody would trust you with a cargo like that.'

'Okay, you bastard,' snarled the Old Man, 'if you get any

closer, we're going to dump some of it in your bloody lap. Just see how you appreciate…'

'You're certainly crazy enough to do it, but as I said, nobody would trust you with…!'

'Get any closer and you'll live to regret it… But not for long. *Over and out.*'

He turned sourly to Angus McKenzie whose merry eyes were all a twinkle and soon a smile played mischievously across his face and he left the radio room sniggering at their private joke, no longer perturbed by the *Judith*'s position. They were both positively glowing with anticipation and, that afternoon, even grabbed some sleep. They awoke to find their warning, as expected, being ignored. The *Judith* was closing in with even more determination.

Shortly after, the ever-vigilant gaze of Captain Anderson saw furtive movement on the aft deck of the *Susan* and strode from the wheelhouse, binoculars at the ready. Angus McKenzie was instantly recognisable, disappearing behind the stern housing with some men. He seemed to have been shouting and gesticulating wildly and his watching eyes narrowed with curiosity. The *Susan* was moving slightly to starboard, placing herself directly ahead of her pursuer's bow. When the engineer and men came back into view, the blood from his face drained rapidly as he watched them lob scarlet canisters over the stern. The vessel ahead began a zigzag course and soon the floating canisters were bobbing over a wide area.

'Christ Almighty!' he gasped, fleeing for the wheelhouse as canisters were flung in all directions. 'THAT CRAZY BASTARD! THAT STUPID, CRAZY BASTARD! HE'LL BLOW US ALL TO HELL! STOP ENGINES! STOP ENGINES!' he bellowed and, turning to the helmsman he yelled 'KEEP CLEAR OF THE EXPLOSIVES!'

'WHERE? WHERE?' he called back, eyes rolling like those of Eddie Cantor.

'THE RED CANISTERS…! KEEP HER CLEAR!'

By the time they discovered they were really painted cocoa

drums, the *Susan Snide* had ploughed way ahead. She couldn't be caught now and no one was more aware of this than her two supremos. Vigorously they pumped each other's arm between warm embraces, thumping backs and digging ribs in childish joy.

'Angus, my dear fellow!' the Old Man gushed, heart brimming with gratitude, 'you are a bloody *marvel! A genius!*'

'Aw...,' he murmured coyly, yet full of pride, '...it was nothin'...'

The Old Man threw back his head and howled in disbelief at such humility. 'Nothing?' he cried. 'Nothing? Why... it was all your *idea*! And it worked like a charm! A bloody marvellous charm!'

Ordinarily he would have been only too eager to follow the *Judith* into port, thus avoiding the obligatory shipboard party, but this was far from ordinary and there would be no party either. He turned away from the engineer, in momentary shame, surveying his hands sheepishly.

'I... er,' he began uncomfortably, shuffling his feet, 'I... er... really didn't mean all those... er... well, disparaging remarks and... er... things, either to your face or in the logbook... er... those charges... loggings... I've erased them all, naturally.'

'Aw, now dinna...'

'Oh Angus,' he sighed, turning to face him, playing with his tie like a contrite Oliver Hardy, ceasing the instant Stanley Stone's likeness to the great comic's partner sprang to mind, 'I honestly didn't mean to...'

'Aw, now dinna fret yersel, mon.' Angus himself was falling victim to the sentiment of the occasion. He laid a reassuring hand on the Old Man's unworthy shoulder, patting it gently. 'There's nae need t' say anymore.'

'No Angus, I've always admitted my mistakes.' The engineer was thinking, 'Like fuck!' but the Old Man wouldn't be silenced. 'I was wrong, Angus, very, very wrong.' He spread out his hands appealingly and spoke in little more than a whisper.

'Could you ever... find it in your generous heart... to again forgive an old, undeserving fool?'

'Aw, now *please...*' Angus begged, taking the Old Man's hand and patting it gently. 'All is forgiven.'

'Good!' the Old Man exclaimed, smiling warmly. 'Rest assured Angus, that my vindictiveness is gone forever. I'm a new man now.' He scratched his chin in reflection. 'Y'know Angus, I think I'll erase all records of the ratings fines... *and* give them all good discharges to boot. What do you think?'

'That'll surprise 'em,' chuckled Angus.

He slipped an arm around the engineer's shoulders, grinning slyly. 'It's... er... not within my jurisdiction, Angus, but... er... if ever I can help in any way with regards to...' he gave his comrade a grateful hug, '...I mean, of course, the shore superintendent engineer's post...' he gave another squeeze. '...I suspect you have designs in that direction, you wily old bugger.'

'Yeah... ah have,' Angus responded with a chuckle, eyes swimming. Like the bosom buddies they never were, they recalled each magnificent moment of their recent triumph in detail, intermingled with outbursts of uncontrollable glee – then a knock on the door heralded the bosun, looking annoyed.

'Yes?' the Old Man chortled, dabbing his eyes. 'What is it?'

'It's the seagulls sir,' he said grimly, and the Old Man exchanged a puzzled glance with Angus McKenzie.

'The seagulls?'

'Yeah.'

After a perplexed silence, the Old Man asked, 'What about the seagulls?'

'They're shitting all over the new paintwork.'

At once the commodores curled up in helpless, delirious laughter which continued until they were gasping for breath and drowning in tears. The engineer staggered out heaving with mirth and the Old Man sent for the cook – company contract no longer worth the paper it was written on – who speechlessly received an order for hand-cream, body lotion, talc and anti-perspirant.

The Old Man spent the next morning soaking in his tub. He preferred it to the shower but its use at sea was governed by the weather. Visions of the morrow's evening, Liverpool and Beatrice, floated tantalizingly before him. She would, he surmised, be somewhat timid at first, which was only to be expected from a virgin bride-to-be upon meeting her betrothed. Yes, quite natural. His approach, therefore, must be gentlemanly and cautious. It would be most improper to expect this sweet, gentle, innocent lady to hop between the sheets at once. He must respect her fragile femininity and besides, such worthy procrastination would enhance her eventual surrender. Softly chuckling in happy anticipation, he reclined, blowing bubbles through his fingers as he dwelt on the forthcoming nuptials, and of a time, not long gone, when all this would have been a pipe dream.

'Come in!' he called in answer to the tap on the door. There followed a spate of incomprehensible mumbling and he raised his voice. 'STICK YOUR BLASTED HEAD IN! I'M NOT A WOMAN!'

'Sir?'

'Oh it's you Sparks.'

'I've had word from Dakar, sir. McCall is out of his coma and is going to pull through.'

'Excellent!' cried the Old Man, bringing the palm of a hand swiftly down to slap the surface of his bath water, sending it splashing all over the sparks. 'Get word to the bosun, I want Able Seaman Neilson up here in about an hour… but don't tell him why.'

The Old Man felt a million dollars when Neilson entered and warily took the proffered seat.

'Cheer up, lad!' he said breezily. 'Great tidings! McCall's out of danger and as soon as he's able to travel he'll be put aboard the next British ship heading home.'

He could clearly see how welcome this was to Neilson who'd suffered ghastly visions of having to break bad news to his sister-in-law. They were both beaming as the Old Man continued. 'The ship will be in Liverpool for about two weeks, discharging cargo and having some engine work done. Now you don't have to leave her there if you don't want to. You can stay aboard, working-by, and then sail to Rotterdam with us. That's where we change from British to foreign crews I'm afraid. So by the time you get back, McCall could well be home.'

Neilson nodded thoughtfully. 'Mmmmmmm, I think I'll *do* that sir. It'll be a bit o' extra money an' wi' companies flaggin' out one after the other, there'll soon be no work left for us.'

The Old Man's brows knit in concern. 'I've no doubt they'll keep a couple of liners under the Red Ensign, just for a bit of a show, but you know what *those* are like lad.'

'Yeah.'

'About a dozen deckhands, a dozen engine hands and five hundred bloody stewards and ancillaries to look after the guests. They're just bloody floating hotels-cum-holiday-camps... not seafaring at all! They've even got ladies HAIRDRESSERS!'

'Yeah.'

'Ever read Masefield?'

'No sir.'

'The crew made seven and twenty dishes,
For the big Jack sharks and little fishes'.

You're all maritime Jack shark victims.'

'Yeah.'

'Yes... and what about that other fellow?'

'What other...?'

'Y'know... he wrote *Doctor at Sea* and *The Captain's Table*. They even made *films* of them.'

'Ah've seen the movies.'

'There you *are* then. *More floating hotel life*... This time through the eyes of a fucking *doctor*!' The Old Man paused – he was digressing. Looking keenly at Neilson, he asked 'What will you do?'

'A shore job, I suppose. What choice *is* there?'

'Doing what?'

'Oh… there's plenty o' boatyards in our area o' Norfolk.'

'There's always the International Pool in Rotterdam.'

Neilson shook his head. 'No good t' either of us sir. Our wives like t' know where we're going' and roughly when we'll be back. From Rotterdam y' c'n get stuck on a tanker not knowin' when y'll ever see 'ome again… ah mean… what kind o' life is that? No Captain… ah think it's the end o' the line for us.'

'But you'll stay on 'til Rotterdam?'

'Yeah.'

'Good. Kindly ask the bosun and the stores if any of the other lads wish to do the same. Tell 'em to leave the names on my desk.'

* * *

The grand arrival at Liverpool was all the Old Man could have wished for. Bunting fluttered in colourful splendour as she came – fresh paint glinting in the sunny March afternoon – proudly to her berth, but all apparently for naught as the Old Man feverishly scanned the quayside.

'Where *is* she? Oh… where *is* she?' he whispered breathlessly to himself. One lady *had* given him a wave of welcome which sent his pounding heart overdriving, but on closer scrutiny she turned into Mrs Duff. There was also the randy wife of the chief engineer of the *Judith.* She had not waved, either in welcome or anything else. The Old Man put this down to her not recognizing him shaven. Yes. That was it. There were dockers waiting to receive the vessel and a couple of men in macs who he took to be agents.

'Ah!' he gasped hopefully as a car drew up, only to groan at the sight of emerging customs officers. Oh it was no good. He descended to main deck level and walked to where the bosun and his men were lowering the gangway, which was also being approached by the Treacle Bender. The Old Man waylaid him.

'Are you going ashore, lad?' he asked.

'Yessir.'

'Bring me back a bottle of whisky, son,' he almost pleaded, having forgotten the last occasion he'd had any. He handed over sufficient money for two. 'You can keep the change only if you do it straight away, before *you* have a drink.'

'I'll be back before y' know it, sir,' he happily replied, and charged off just as the second mate came into view.

'Ah Mr Camp!' the Old Man exclaimed, 'doing anything important?'

'Just off to the phone box sir.'

'Can it wait half an hour or so?'

'Well… yes… I suppose…'

'Good.' The Old Man thrust the photograph into his hands. 'If this lady appears, she is to be conducted at once to my quarters.'

Hercules Duff had been detailed to attend the agent while the Old Man, a bent and sorry figure, shuffled back to his cabin alone. To his further annoyance, the agent was there awaiting him – a peculiar-looking chap in an extra-long mackintosh. He had an obscenely large nose protruding from a hirsute face beneath a trilby-hiding forehead. Displeased by his presence, the Old Man waved a weary arm towards the door.

'Look,' he said, 'the first officer is dealing with…'

'Crawley?' came a tentative squeak.

'Huh?' he gasped, instantly alert – the hairs tingling on the back of his neck. His heart was thudding madly in his ears. 'Er… Wha…?'

'Are you… Crawley?'

He stared transfixed at the figure before him, who repeated the question.

'Y…y…yes,' he stammered, in a trance. 'I'm Crawley.'

He watched thunderstruck as mackintosh and facial disguise were discarded. She flew into his arms, his mouth gaped wide, as she sobbed and trembled, ravenously biting his neck as he quivered uncontrollably where he stood.

'Oh…' he managed at last. 'Oh… Beatrice…' he breathed into her ear, 'is it really you?'

It really was. She had mislaid his photo weeks previously and half forgotten what he looked like but his correspondence had kept the ship and Liverpool firmly in her mind. They were married the following day by special licence and spent two weeks of pampered luxury at the Adelphe Hotel (where a private cot was provided for Tedward). It was here he began work on his autobiography entitled, 'The Old Man Cometh.' It was never completed. They then returned to the *Fu-King Susan,* to sail the seas and oceans of the world in conjugal bliss, with crews unable to speak a work of English and praying to Mecca five times daily. And so they lived happily ever after.

And if, as they say, you believe that…

The British Merchant Navy
R.I.P.
FINISHED WITH ENGINES